TO LOVE ANOTHER DAY

The Memoirs of
CORY AQUINO

From The Years of Trials, Tragedy and Transformation (1972-1986)

Compiled and Edited by Rapa Lopa
with Rhona Lopa-Macasaet and Paolo R. Reyes

TO LOVE ANOTHER DAY

The Memoirs of
CORY AQUINO

From The Years of Trials, Tragedy and Transformation (1972-1986)

Compiled and Edited by Rapa Lopa
with Rhona Lopa-Macasaet and Paolo R. Reyes

Praise for
To Love Another Day: The Memoirs of Cory Aquino

"Anyone who has read hagiography or the lives of the saints will know that tears and prayers form the arsenal of the canonized. Most of them will offer the other cheek when unjustly slapped, while you and I will do what is natural and hit back — harder. Presidents of the Philippines, especially the current one, like to project power and strength, so tears and prayers are not in their vocabulary — and that is what made Corazon C. Aquino unusual. . . . When she stepped out of Malacañang, Cory was often asked to write her memoirs, to leave her version of history. She attempted to do so in 1996, drafting stray recollections, and then got stalled. . . . Fortunately, Rapa Lopa has published the 1996 recollections. . . . it is not an autobiography. Not a chronological retelling of a life, identifying significant events from birth to twilight. . . . *To Love Another Day* is an engaging and inspiring read. . . . It is, at best, a teaser, edited with the soft lens of Lopa's idealized image of his saintly aunt."

Ambeth Ocampo,
historian and *Philippine Daily Inquirer* columnist

"The significance of Cory's book cannot be overemphasized. Her stature alone lends it the poundage of truth needed to crush the creeping conspiracy to not only distort, but flat-out falsify the history of the period to rehabilitate its villains. . . . Actually, Cory's book, published 10 years after her death, could not have arrived better-timed: A Marcos idolater has come to power and been quick to embrace his idol's dynastic descendants; together, they are now inventing a grand and redeeming Marcos legacy. Cory's recollections are here to set it right. They resound in the details, where the devil is particularly recognizable in his pettiness."

Vergel O. Santos,
journalist and Rappler columnist

"You can read *To Love Another Day* in one sitting. It is a heartfelt narration of Cory Aquino's years of trials, tragedy and change, from 1972, when Pres. Ferdinand Marcos declared martial law, to 1986, when she was swept into the presidency. The book reveals some details we have not heard before. Young adults will be able to relate to this book, as if they were listening to the voice of an aunt who is telling them the stories of her time in clear and vivid prose. And it can make you laugh and cry as the book packs powerful memories of the cruelty of martial law interspersed with a sense of humor that helped a woman, thrust into the unexpected, cope."

Marites Dañguilan Vitug,
journalist and Rappler editor-at-large

"And I thought I knew her enough. However, *To Love Another Day* offers us a rare and privileged glimpse of the innermost thoughts, sentiments and convictions of Tita Cory and a broader understanding of the events and characters that shaped our nation. . . . As we encounter a Tita Cory giddy and self-conscious during her initial foray into political campaigns, and resilient and impregnable in the face of the assassination of Ninoy and the numerous coups staged during her tenure as president, we are bemused and inspired, moved to tears and filled with hope. An all-too-human Cory makes us realize that patriotism is our call, too, and heroism within our reach."

Fr. Manoling Francisco, S.J.,
theology professor and composer

TABLE OF CONTENTS

PREFACE

It was Fr. Catalino Arevalo, S.J., the eminent Jesuit theologian and Auntie Cory's spiritual adviser, who first planted the seed of an idea for a new book to retell the story of Auntie Cory and Uncle Ninoy.

In 2010, about a year after Auntie Cory's death, I had several conversations with Father Arevalo, where we both shared our own reflections on how she and Uncle Ninoy touched our lives. Each time we exchanged stories, he would encourage me to share my personal recollections with others and to publish a small book. Each time, I promised him that I would do so.

Then in his homily on August 21, 2013, entitled "The Faith of Martyrs: Remembering Ninoy and Cory," Father Arevalo singled out one of our conversations. He recounted how I thought the story of Ninoy and Cory Aquino must be told: "It must be grasped as a love story, the story of the special love they held in their hearts, perhaps a unique love, in all of our history, for our people and our country."

Since that time, the idea of publishing a book about Auntie Cory and Uncle Ninoy has nagged at me.

My hesitation in all these years, however, arose not only from the doubts I had over my writing abilities, but also from another, more sensitive issue that was haunting my conscience.

Sometime in October 2007, my team in the Aquino Foundation was planning to create the Cory Aquino website that would serve as her official online portal. In the course of our brainstorming, we realized that she was going to be celebrating her seventy-fifth birthday on January

25, 2008. Anticipating this milestone, we thought that it would be an opportune time to collect letters and tributes from her friends and relatives, which we could then compile and upload to her website. To this end, we sought out these friends and relatives and gave them strict instructions to keep this project a secret, since we intended it to be a surprise for Auntie Cory.

A month later, on November 26, 2007, to be exact, my team and I were having a lunch meeting when my phone suddenly rang. It was a call from "Azon," the proxy name of Auntie Cory in my phone directory. I excused myself, quickly stepped out of the restaurant, and answered the call, "Yes, Auntie Cory, what can I do for you?"

"What is this I hear that you are asking for letters from people to write to me?" she asked in a somewhat irritated tone of voice.

Stunned and surprised that she had found out about our secret project, I could not immediately reply.

"Whatever it is, Rapa, *tigil-tigilan mo na 'yan!*" she continued, admonishing me to halt this project once and for all.

"Yes, Auntie Cory," was all I could say, and then she hung up.

Blood rushed to my head, and I felt terrible that I had displeased and upset her. Those who knew Auntie Cory can very well understand how dismaying it was to be out of her good graces, especially when one disappointed her or betrayed her trust.

So, feeling much troubled, I went back to our meeting and told the team, "*Patay, alam na ni* Auntie Cory *'yung plano natin!*" We'd been found out, and she wasn't pleased.

I knew we were going to see each other later that day, as we were both attending the birthday celebration of Auntie Josephine Reyes, her older sister, at the Wack Wack Golf and Country Club. It goes without saying that my anxiety levels kept escalating as the evening drew closer.

When I finally arrived in Wack Wack and greeted her, she quietly pulled me aside and asked me what my crazy idea was all about. I explained that it was meant to be a surprise tribute for her seventy-fifth birthday, and we thought that it would be nice for her to know what other people felt about her.

All she said was, "Rapa, let us not bother people anymore about things like that. That is not important. Let's just focus on doing our work in the foundation."

I replied, "Yes, Auntie Cory, I'm sorry about this." And that was the last we spoke of this incident.

If there is one thing I learned about Auntie Cory from that incident, however, it is how detached she was from the need to be recognized, affirmed, praised, and glorified. Therefore, knowing this, I wondered if she would approve of my calling attention to her through this book. The last thing I would want is for Auntie Cory to visit me in my dreams to deliver the same disapproving message: "Rapa, *tigil-tigilan mo na 'yan!*"

Truthfully, I struggled in deciding whether or not to put this book together. On the one hand, there was Auntie Cory's detachment from, and distaste of, things that intentionally focused attention on her and purposely invited praise towards her. On the other, there was the unwavering encouragement from Father Arevalo, who sincerely believes that their love story needs to be told.

Then I recalled a moment in 1996, when Auntie Cory told me that she had already started writing her autobiography. It was meant to be a tell-all book about her life's journey. I think there was a part of her that *did* want to look back on the past and document significant events in her life. However, again, being the person that she was, I felt her purpose for writing her life story was not so much to draw attention towards her, but to establish the facts and share the lessons she had learned along the way.

Although she had written some drafts, she had not yet put down on paper everything that she wanted to say. I suggested, therefore that it might help if we videotaped her recollections in a series of interview sessions, where she could narrate everything she remembered. After, we could have the interviews transcribed to help her progress with her drafts.

So in July of 1996, we arranged these sessions together with my cousin, writer Rhona Lopa-Macasaet, Ate Ballsy Aquino-Cruz, my executive assistant Amor Castillo, and Mang Johnny Amores (the cameraman of TV producer Maria Montelibano). In these never-before-seen video recordings, we managed to capture her remembrances, stories from the declaration of martial law up to the EDSA People Power Revolution, the narrative of significant events in her life.

Moreover, together with my other cousin, director Jun Reyes, and Ben Tangco (one of her post-presidency speech writers), we were also able to interview her for two audio-visual projects of the foundation. First was *The Candle of Our Lives,* the launch video for the Ninoy and Cory Aquino Leadership Center, which was sponsored by Drs. Roland and Rosalinda Hortaleza. This was followed by the 2009 documentary, *The Last Journey of Ninoy,* which featured her final interview before she passed on. These two video interviews provided us with more material, more stories and insights, which we also transcribed.

Initially, I envisioned this book to be a collection of short essays I would write around specific themes gathered from Auntie Cory's narrations, as I have recently done. These short essays about her and Uncle Ninoy have, in fact, been posted to social media and reprinted in the *Philippine Daily Inquirer* (thanks to my dear friend, Thelma S. San Juan). In these essays, I recounted stories and anecdotes of my personal encounters with them (but more with Auntie Cory) and included my insights and reflections stemming from these encounters.

However, as I read through the original transcripts of the interviews, I worried that I would overlook very important details if I picked a mere line or two and quoted only portions of her transcribed accounts. I felt there was a need to relay the stories of Auntie Cory in full, so that we can thoroughly grasp what was clearly the most pivotal, defining, and transformative period of Uncle Ninoy's and Auntie Cory's lives.

Then it dawned on me—who best to tell their story than Auntie Cory herself?

If I felt a sense of relief at the realization that this book would require very little writing on my part, I also sincerely believe that I would not have anyway been able to fully capture their story if I had attempted to write it myself.

So let me therefore present this book, which is really Auntie Cory's unpublished memoirs of a small chapter of her life—a little over thirteen years, to be specific—narrated in her candid, unadorned, yet evocative, prose.

This is the story of her life-changing choices that were closely intertwined with her country and people's history. It is her story of vulnerability, courage, and fidelity, of enduring hope and steadfast faith, of which we Filipinos were all very much a part, perhaps without many of us even being aware of it. It is a story, I think, that holds relevance up to this day, during these dark and divisive times.

This is her story that I've been so blessed and privileged to have witnessed up close and that still constantly accompanies me on my ongoing life journey. It always gives me hope when I fall into despair. It humbles me when I feel entitled. It gives me courage when I am paralyzed by fear. It inspires me to be more compassionate when I am tempted to be indifferent. But more than anything, it moves me to love whenever it is most difficult to do so.

This is Uncle Ninoy and Auntie Cory's love story.

But it is as much mine as it is yours.

RAPA LOPA
Pasay City, 2019

INTRODUCTION
by Rapa Lopa

Much has been written about the enduring narrative of Ninoy and Cory Aquino and the unique role they played in Philippine history. Thus, the idea of publishing another book about them was really quite daunting.

The retelling of our country's history will always have its complexities and complications. There will always be many-sided viewpoints about the relevance and importance of past events, depending on the perspectives of those who are able to live long enough to write their stories.

Since Auntie Cory did not live long enough to share their story in the manner she would have wanted to, I needed to be mindful that her compiled recollections in this book were edited from my own perspective and not hers.

The interviews we conducted, which were the main source of the stories included in this book, were very much like a dialogue, a typical conversation you would have with her. We would ask her a question that would prompt her to recall, in vivid detail, private anecdotes about the past. The stories she shared were informal, free flowing, and would sometimes jump from one subject matter to another.

The challenge, for us, was how to weave the loose and casual style of her storytelling into more readable and coherent narratives, without compromising the essence and accuracy of what she wanted to say.

More than a mere rehash of history, the primary intention of this book is to help Filipinos remember and learn from the powerful and compelling tale of two people who found themselves catapulted into the eye of the country's political storm and how they weathered the challenges that fate had thrust upon them.

Given the intimate nature of these memoirs, I also invite you, dear readers, to go beyond the historical facts and chronological sequence of events, as we are wont to do when reading history books. Instead, embed yourself in her stories, imagine yourself in the unfolding scene, and be sensitive to your emotions and feelings as you do so.

Ask yourself, "If I were Cory or Ninoy or any of the characters, how would I have reacted? How would I have responded? What decisions would I have made if I were in their shoes?"

This exercise is what my Jesuit mentors refer to as the Ignatian Contemplation or Imagination. In his book, *The Jesuit Guide to (Almost) Everything: A Spirituality for Real Life*, Fr. James Martin, SJ, wrote that this Ignatian tradition of prayer was popularized by St. Ignatius of Loyola, who put it center stage in his *Spiritual Exercises*, where he called it "composition of place."

Father Martin expounds that "in Ignatian contemplation, one is told to 'compose the place' by imagining yourself in a scene from the Bible, or in God's presence, and then taking part in it. It's a way of allowing God to speak to you through your imagination."

When Father Martin first encountered this method of prayer, he expressed his skepticism and confessed his doubts about the whole idea to a fellow Jesuit, the late Fr. David Fleming, who helped him make sense of it.

After their conversation, Father Martin concluded that "using our imagination wasn't so much making things up, as it was trusting our imagination as a way to lead us to the one who created it: God. This didn't mean that everything we imagine during prayer is coming from

God. But, rather, it means that from time to time God could use our imagination as a way to communicate with us."

I offer this approach in reading this book because I feel that there is a strong parallel between the Gospel narratives and the narratives shared by Auntie Cory. Both are historical recollections; both have stories of human beings choosing to immerse themselves in the struggles of fellow human beings; both have stories of vulnerabilities, trials, and sufferings; both have stories of victories and failures; both have stories of love.

Reading the final manuscript of this book before submitting it to the publisher, I once again immersed myself in Uncle Ninoy and Auntie Cory's story of love, while adopting the practice of Ignatian contemplation. By doing so, I gained new insights that I never had before, remembered old lessons that I realized I was no longer too heedful of and that I needed to commit to live by, as time and again I resolved to become my better self. These personal reflections I humbly impart in the epilogue of this book.

I certainly hope you enjoy reading *To Love Another Day* as much as I enjoyed putting it together.

Chapter I
Arrest & Imprisonment
1972 – 1979

God had other plans

It is true, to a certain extent, that our fate is in our hands. We make choices, commit acts, speak words that decide the direction our lives should take. And yet, on occasion, events intrude of which we have no control and our plans go awry, our lives drastically change. It was that way with Ninoy and me.

Before September 23, 1972, it seemed that there was nothing that he could not handle. He had planned his life and everything was going on schedule. At that time, the important event he was most looking forward to was the forthcoming presidential elections of 1973.

However, God, I guess, had other plans for him.

On the evening of September 23, 1972, Pres. Ferdinand Marcos declared martial law. It was a grim-looking Kit Tatad, information minister, who made the announcement on TV. Marcos had signed Proclamation 1081, a proclamation that was supposedly signed as early as September 21, but was only made public two days later.

In the weeks before, there had already been rumors of martial law. And in the hushed and secret conversations among the citizenry was an undercurrent of dread, a dread that was made real on that evening of September 23. All of a sudden, it seemed, a great shroud of silence fell all across the country. There were no commercial radio broadcasts, the screens on televisions went blank, the streets emptied. Everyone then knew what had happened, but no one knew what it meant, how lives would shift, futures be reshaped.

For us, without our being aware of it, our lives had begun to radically shift even before this announcement was made. It all began with the news on television that Johnny Ponce Enrile, Marcos's minister of defense, had been ambushed on the evening of September 22. My immediate thought was to call Ninoy at the Hilton Hotel, where they were conducting the last meetings of the Committee on Tariff, of which he was a member. When I spoke to him, I expressed my concern that the authorities might pin the blame for the ambush of Enrile on him.

Then, on September 23, with the day just beginning, I received a call from Ninoy. He informed me that he was on his way to Camp Crame. I was perplexed because he could not tell me why, but he assured me that I would know eventually.

Later, I received a call from Judy Roxas, wife of Sen. Gerry Roxas. She asked me if I knew what had happened to Ninoy. When I told her no, she informed me that Sen. John Osmeña had just called from the Hilton. Martial law had been declared, he said, and Ninoy had been arrested. Judy also said that Gerry was on his way to Crame and would call us once he got to see or talk to Ninoy.

I woke my children up (at that time Kris was only a year-and-a-half old) to tell them what had happened; and when I told them, I couldn't help but cry.

I remember the flurry of phone calls that followed, calls from people greatly worried, like my sister, Terry, and her husband, Baby Lopa, who asked me what I planned to do. I also talked to my brother, Peping, who suggested that we move out of our house in Times Street, Quezon City, and to our parents' house in Forbes Park, Makati. Monching Mitra also called and asked me where Ninoy was. When I told him that Ninoy had been arrested and brought to Crame, Monching knew his own arrest was coming. Apparently, his dogs had been barking and, true enough, soon after there were the military to pick him up.

Gerry, who had gotten back to his house at about two-thirty in the morning, called next. He had gone to Crame to see Ninoy. He said that Ninoy had also suggested we move out of the house in the meantime.

Stopping first at Gerry's house in Cubao, I asked him whether or not I could visit Ninoy that day. He could not give me an answer, but encouraged me to try. In Gerry's house at that time was Chino Roces. Nap Rama may have also been there. They were biding their time, waiting to be arrested, certain that the military would come for them soon. In fact, Pacita Roces, Chino's wife, had earlier warned Chino not to come home. The military had already been to their house looking for him.

My children and I then proceeded to my parents' house in Forbes. As we made our way there, I thought how everything seemed so strangely calm and peaceful. There was nothing on the radio except music, and I thought, No one knows what is going on.

When we got to Forbes, Baby and Terry were already there, as well as another sister, Passy Teopaco, who lived with my parents then. We were all quite at a loss what to do, not knowing from whom to seek help or even any bit of information. I remember calling Joe Rojas, a friend of Ninoy's, to inform him about Ninoy's arrest and ask if he could help. I told him, *"Kinulong na si Ninoy."*

Needless to say, sleep was impossible. I must have gone to sleep around three o'clock or four o'clock in the morning. I would retreat to the bathroom and cry. I had no inkling what was going to happen: What was to become of Ninoy? What was to become of my children and me?

Then at six that morning, Tessie Oreta, my sister-in-law, called to offer to accompany me to Crame. She had already been there before and had experience with this sort of thing, when her husband, Len Oreta, was arrested and detained in 1971 during the suspension of the writ of habeas corpus.

In Crame, after introducing myself to the authorities there, Tessie and I were brought to what looked like the camp's gymnasium. I was told that

I would not be allowed to speak to Ninoy, only to wave at him. When I finally saw Ninoy, we waved at each other, as instructed, and that was it. Tessie and I were then led away.

Back in Forbes, Lupita Kashiwahara, another sister-in-law, told me that Preciosa Soliven, the wife of Max Soliven, had been able to get permission from Gen. Eddie Ramos to visit Max, and that perhaps I could ask for the same.

When I was finally granted the visit, Ninoy told me that he and the others were going to be transferred to Fort Bonifacio. The following morning, a Sunday, Nena Diokno, wife of Sen. Pepe Diokno; Toto Locsin, wife of Teddy Locsin, Sr.; Pacita, and I went there to inquire about the procedures for visiting our husbands. Finally, we were allowed to see them that same day.

Before going in to see our husbands, we had to be bodily searched by WACs (Women's Auxiliary Corps). The whole experience was so absolutely new and unsettling. At that time, I was in a state of disbelief: how unbelievable it was that these things could happen or be done to a senator, publishers of a newspaper and a national magazine. Imagine what they could do to ordinary people, who wield neither influence nor power.

Still in the beginning, things did not seem too bad. We could visit every day for an hour, although there was always a WAC and a military soldier looking on.

At that time, Ninoy and the others did not think that the worst had happened yet. The situation was still tolerable for Ninoy because at least they were all together. Besides him, there were Pepe, Soc, and Monching, the senators; Chino and Teddy, the publishers; Max, Jose Mari Velez, and Nap, the columnists; and Voltaire Garcia, a student activist.

As they tried to adapt as best they could to prison life, they shared chores, taking turns washing the dishes and doing other mundane tasks.

Sometimes, a psychologist came to talk them. I doubt, however, if he was of any help to them at all because, for one, Teddy absolutely refused to talk to him. And Chino, when he did, "confided" to him such things as how he was falling in love with the goats roaming around Fort Bonifacio. Ninoy, on the other hand, always welcomed the opportunity to talk.

Soc had his very own nightly ritual as well. Every night, he would make it a point to bathe with a *tabo* (dipper) and change into a clean shirt. They found this a source of amusement and always teased him, asking, where are you going?

Soc had also suggested that they pray the rosary every night. It was he, in fact, who taught Ninoy the Glorious mysteries. And so they took turns leading the rosary every night.

The thing that struck me most about Soc was his serenity. For this is what I observed about him, that, in spite of the predicament they were in, he had this air of calm about him. Confined to their cells, amid all that restless energy, the speculations, the worries, he seemed nonetheless to radiate an inner peace. Soc really had a good influence on all of them because of that inner peace.

If Soc was their religious instructor, Teddy was their resident poet. He was well-versed in poetry and gave them lessons on it. But most of the time, of course, they discussed politics and when they were going to be released. Ninoy, as early as then, volunteered to them that he felt he would be the last of them to be released.

It was, I imagine, an unusual and very interesting setting, where all of them were more or less intellectually compatible and so could carry on discussions about everything under the sun. Between the mysteries of the rosary, the elements of poetry, and the all-consuming topic of politics, the exchange of ideas must have been very stimulating.

At the same time, however, it also spelled a total change in their lives. Here were some of the country's most influential people all at once made ineffective under the complete control of the military authorities. Yet the situation also enabled them to get to know each other better. Without the trappings of their powerful positions, suddenly they were all on the same level. Thrown together, as they were, for seventy days, they became familiar with each other's quirks and habits, as well as points of character, good and bad.

Then on December 1, 1972, Chino, Teddy, and Nap were released, and two more were released on December 4.

As it turned out, Ninoy and Pepe were to be left behind in jail.

The crumpled paper

The following year—February 1973, in particular—turned out to be an even more distressing time for us all. Ninoy had been prohibited from communicating with anyone. Impatient about not being able to make contact with anybody, he began then to scribble notes and messages that we, of course, had to spirit out for him. He apparently had already devised a scheme, needing nothing more than candy wrappers.

We were now instructed to bring him hard candies every time we came to visit. He would then type his messages single space on onion-skin sheets, cramming in as much information as he could, roll up these sheets nice and tight, and conceal them in the candy wrappers. Ninoy was confident that we would not be found out. The security men could not know any differently just by looking at them because, unless they held them in their hands and felt their unusual lightness, they most certainly looked like candies. Also, the fact that Kris was still young at the time, they most likely figured that, like most kids, she simply loved candies. There was no cause for suspicion, and our secret operations went smoothly for a time.

It is not to say, however, that we never had any close calls. One time, Ninoy had this very long message to be spirited out and he asked Ballsy to retrieve it from the bathroom in the visiting area. For the first time, however, we were searched on our way out, whereas before we were searched only upon coming in. I was completely caught off guard, but had the presence of mind to express my surprise out loud, and I exclaimed, actually to warn the others, that there was a new procedure and that we would be searched again. My heart was racing because I knew that Ballsy was carrying this message, three or four pages long, that she just had enough time to crumple into balls and mix up with the Kleenex tissues in her hand. When the WAC asked Ballsy to empty out her pockets, she even opened her hands like it was the most natural thing to do. I suppose that if you have no idea what it is you are looking for, you will not be suspicious of anything, least of all everyday, commonplace things.

Ninoy specifically wrote this message for Bob Shaplen, who was with the *New Yorker* at the time, and Alfonso Policarpio, one of Ninoy's friends in the Senate. He had instructed me to send this message to them, and so I did. I did not know, however, that Ninoy had told Poli to make copies of this message available to foreign correspondents, and that Poli had, accordingly, sent one to the *Bangkok Post.* I also was not aware that this saw print there.

Then on February 23, I was curtly told by the Fort Bonifacio authorities that my visiting privileges were suspended and I could not see Ninoy. They could not tell me when I could see him again.

Had we been found out? As soon as I could, I made an appointment to see Undersec. Mike Barbero, the deputy minister of defense then and my *compaɩre,* to ask him if he could help me. It was only then that things became clear to me. Apparently, Ninoy's message had seen print. In the end, Mike could only advise me to tell Ninoy to refrain from such activities.

And from February 23 to April 8, we did not see Ninoy and had no idea what had happened to him.

Then one day, one of Ninoy's former security guards, a member of the Police Constabulary (PC), came to see me. He narrated this long story to me about how he had seen Ninoy in Fort Bonifacio, even describing how forlorn he looked. As it turned out, the day that he told me he saw Ninoy in Fort Bonifacio, Ninoy was actually already in Fort Magsaysay, in Laur, Nueva Ecija! And there I was, feeling very grateful to this man; and I even offered him a little something in appreciation for this bit of, what I thought, valuable news, but was actually false information. That was a first lesson in my life.

It was only that I was anxious for any information, eager to find out what was going on. My sisters-in-law, Lupita and Tessie, even went so far as to consult a *manghuhula*, a fortuneteller who "revealed" to them that Ninoy was being held captive in a far-off island somewhere. In other words, we all were just trying to seek and gather any information wherever we could.

It was most agonizing, not only for me, but for Nena as well. She had also been barred from seeing Pepe and, like me with Ninoy, had had no contact with him in all this time.

What worried me also was that Ninoy had no money. Ninoy had refused to take any cash, saying what would he need it for, what could he possibly buy inside Fort Bonifacio. He had only his checkbook with him, and so I requested the people in First United Bank to please honor any checks that might be issued by him. Nena, however, reassured me that Pepe did have cash because she would leave him small amounts during their conjugal visits. On all our previous visits, we had also brought boxes and boxes of canned goods, and it was a consoling thought that they would have enough supplies to sustain them for quite a while.

At this time, Sen. Lorenzo Tañada suggested to Nena and me that we go to the Supreme Court to appeal to them that, for humanitarian considerations, we be allowed to visit our husbands. We went to the Supreme Court on a Friday, April 6, and during the proceedings where we presented our appeal, the defense, headed by Estelito Mendoza, stated to our amazement that the problem with Nena and me was that we were always speaking in code. This, it turned out, was their chief complaint against us! But speaking in code was something that we had learned to do because there was always a camera present during our visits. The circumstances had necessitated it. We had names for Imelda Marcos, the officer, and even ourselves. Ninoy called himself Micah and I was Judith, names we picked from the Bible.

Eventually, the Supreme Court decided in our favor and, for humanitarian considerations, the judges requested—not directed, but *requeste*—the military to allow us to visit our husbands. At this point, however, we still did not know that they were in Fort Magsaysay. They still had not told us where they were.

All this time, we thought that they were in Fort Bonifacio. So, Saturday morning, the very next day, Nena and I went to Fort Bonifacio to inquire from a colonel there when we could see our husbands. We waited all morning, and did not get to see this colonel until after lunch.

Nena and I were ushered into his office separately. When it was my turn, he opened the conversation by telling me that the problem with Filipino men is that they have all these women on the side. He then showed me letters, purportedly written by Ninoy to his "lover," that he said he had transcribed. My first thought was, why transcribe them when I can very well read Ninoy's handwriting? He went on and on in this way, implying all kinds of sordid things, and so I interrupted him and asked if this was all he was going to tell me. If so, then I was going to leave. Things of that nature I only discussed with my husband, I told him, and then I stood up and left. Maur Lichauco, another sister-in-law, who was waiting outside, saw that there was such great anger written on my face, and she and Nena asked me what happened. I told them that these people are just playing around with us. These people are very good at using psychological warfare.

I went to see Senator Tañada and told him what had happened. Apparently, they had also tried the same strategy with the other wives. I suppose they aimed to cause friction between husband and wife, so that the wife, perhaps out of anger and disgust, would be provoked to talk. I was right, he said, to not have put importance on what the colonel said, but that I must be prepared for worse things.

Laur

The following day, Sunday, April 8, Nena and I were called to go to Fort Bonifacio. There, we talked to Col. Josephus Ramas and no longer to Lt. Col. Pedro Villalon, who was really terrible. Colonel Ramas informed us that, after lunch, they would take us to see our husbands and that helicopters were already on standby. I wondered about this. Why use helicopters? Aren't they here in Fort Bonifacio? But then Ninoy had also always impressed upon me the vast size of Fort Bonifacio, that it was more than a thousand hectares in area, and I thought that maybe they were being held in some remote corner of it. Colonel Ramas was still being vague, even up to this point, and would only admit that they were just a little way from where we were. In any case, however, I told him that we would not be able to fit in the helicopters, as I had my five children with me, plus the *yaya* of the youngest, and Nena, her ten.

We decided, instead, to go in our cars and, as a safety measure, Passy and Maur would follow us in their cars, in case they brought us somewhere or something happened to us. However, at a gas station, where we stopped to wait for the other vehicles, I thought better of it and asked Passy and Maur to go back home. I was afraid the military would resent the idea of having other people trail us and therefore change their minds about allowing us to see our husbands.

When we passed the tollgates to the North Expressway, I began to wonder where we were really going. My hope was that the people we passed on the road would remember seeing us at such and such a time or day, that, in case we were suddenly made to disappear from the face of the earth, at least someone would be able to say that they saw us.

It took us three hours to get to our destination. And it was only when we arrived there that we learned we were in Fort Magsaysay, Laur, Nueva Ecija.

The place reminded me of a scene from the movie *Bridge on the River Kwai*, because of all the rolled barbed wire and outposts and soldiers with dogs. There was *sawali* (mats of woven bamboo strips used as partitions) all around. Someone led us to a room and, upon entering, Nena and I gave each other a look of incredulity because hanging in the room was a painting of a nude woman.

Then we were instructed that the Dioknos would go see Pepe first and have thirty minutes with him, after which it would be our turn to see Ninoy. At the end of their thirty minutes with Pepe, the Dioknos came back and they were all in tears. We were startled and surprised at this because we always knew the Dioknos to be very brave—*matapang*—and not the type who easily cry.

They told my children that they would not even be able to kiss their dad. And when we went to see Ninoy, we saw why. Chicken-wire fences separated us from each other—one fence in front of us and, two feet away, another fence in front of him. A photographer behind us and a photographer behind him took pictures constantly. Ninoy looked awful. His hair had grown long and he was holding his pants up because he had lost a considerable amount of weight.

When he saw us, Ninoy started to cry. This was the first time, ever, that I saw him looking so defeated and helpless. My daughters could do nothing but cry as well. Only Noynoy and I managed not to cry. I was strong, or seemed that way, because earlier, before we left, I had asked Passy to give me a tranquilizer to calm my nerves, and she handed me one that I thought was what Dr. Pepot San Gabriel used to prescribe. But instead of taking a Librium 5, I apparently had taken a Librium 10! Which I thought was just as well, because I did not want to give the military authorities the satisfaction of seeing me in tears. This was one triumph, small though it was, that I was determined to deny them.

All this time, he did not know that he was in Fort Magsaysay. I, on my part, assumed that he knew. He asked how we got there and I related to him how Senator Tañada had helped us get permission from the Supreme Court to see him, and how after all those weeks we were finally granted the chance.

Ninoy then suggested that, in case we did not see each other again, we should pray the rosary every night at eight o'clock. This would ensure that we would all be praying together as a family. (Now that I think about it, he was not allowed to wear a watch, so how could he know if it was already eight o'clock?)

It did seem like a last good-bye, as he told Noynoy, being the only boy in the family, that he would now have to take care of his sisters and me. This was the first and only time I saw Ninoy lose hope. He just wanted an end to it all ("*Gusto ko ng tapusin.*"), seeing how difficult it was not just for him but for the family as well. This was so unlike him, who could do anything and everything.

But in the midst of this distressing situation, what did my husband tell me? Ninoy informed me that we had some outstanding debts for which we still needed to pay the banks. You would think that for what could have been his farewell message it would be more dramatic! But there I was listening to my husband telling me the bleak news of how much we owed.

Then Ballsy encouraged him not to give up, and, in his diary, he wrote that what Ballsy said had meant so much to him. He also wrote that he was so ashamed of himself for breaking down, because there I was so brave and in full control of myself (because of the Librium!).

It was getting late, close to seven in the evening, when our visit ended. We asked Lt. Voltaire Gazmin (colonel, later on), who was Ninoy's godson in marriage, if we could stay the night, as the drive back would be long and tiring. He had no authority to decide on such matters, however, since the one in charge was Lt. Felix Bueno (who was really not *bueno* at all). Lieutenant Bueno said that no, the orders were for us to go back home.

On the way home, Nena's van broke down. While waiting for repairs to be done, I decided to go over to her to chat, but I was not even allowed to do that. I was ordered to go back to my car and stay there.

Nena and I had forgotten to ask our husbands if they had any cash. But I had brought a*obo* and some sheets, because I did not know what to expect. Ninoy and Pepe shared the a*obo*, divided it between the two of them. But they never got to see or talk to each other.

It was past midnight when we reached home. I immediately called my father, who had worried about us all day, to say that we were home now and safe. The following morning, all the tears that I had held back kept falling and falling. Every time I would retell my story, I would cry. We really thought that that was the end, that our meeting the previous day was truly the last.

Soon after our visit to Ninoy, Ballsy had a dream. She recalled that, in her dream, her dad had a message, and this message was specific that from now on our new code would be "the palm of our hands." We wondered, what did that mean?

Two weeks after, just before Easter, I visited Marilita Osmeña, the first wife of Serge, who himself was detained in Fort Bonifacio. She was still allowed to visit Serge, and I think Chita Lopez was also still allowed to visit her husband Geny. I asked if there was any news about Ninoy that she might have heard from Serge. She told me that Serge and the others had been expressly ordered not to say anything about Ninoy and Pepe, or have anything to do with them in any way. Otherwise, they too would lose their visiting privileges and suffer the same consequences. Nonetheless, she had dared asked Serge about Ninoy that morning when she went to visit him. But since they could not mention his name out loud, she traced with her finger, on the palm of her hand, the letters of Ninoy's name. Then she signed to him if Ninoy was there, in Fort Bonifacio, and Serge nodded yes.

When I got home, I told Ballsy, "This is what your dream meant."

Quality time found in detention

We were finally allowed to see Ninoy again that Easter Sunday. My mother-in-law was able to come with us, and Ballsy, in spite of suffering from a severe stomachache, decided to go as well. It felt good to see Ninoy, but at the same time it was depressing.

I had so many things weighing on my mind and in the midst of all this, my father noticed that Ballsy, who was then staying with him and my mother in Forbes and slept in their room, was just lying there looking very weak. He called Dr. Ricardo de Guzman to check on her, and it turned out that the stomachache was due to appendicitis. She must have borne the pain all day with all the fortitude she could muster. Not wanting to worry me further, my parents decided against telling me that surgery had to be performed that very night. When I eventually found out, I was thankful that the surgery had been successful and that everything had turned out all right. It's as if we didn't already have enough problems!

Two weeks after this incident, we were allowed to visit Ninoy again. I knew that they were going to be very strict with us, and I was concerned that the military authorities would be suspicious of Ballsy and her bandages, that they might think we were trying to smuggle something in again. This time, however, we were hardly even searched. We puzzled over this, but soon saw the reason why. There was no need for searches because they had put up chicken-wire fences again, inside Fort Bonifacio, to separate Ninoy from us.

Seeing this, Kris told her *yaya*, "*Parang nasa* zoo *ang* daddy. *Hindi na puezeng mag*-kiss." She thought of him as being in a cage, like animals in the zoo. At her young age, that was what struck her most.

Ninoy was proud of how the children held up during those difficult years and was grateful for all the sacrifices they had to endure for his sake. Growing up under such unusual circumstances, the children realized how different we were from other families. Their friends hardly talked about politics, maybe because they were warned not to talk about Marcos. Still, I felt very appreciative when a number of them went to the house the day after martial law was declared in a show of support for my children. My friends did not come until later. I guess, when you're young, you don't worry as much about the consequences.

Ninoy and I made it a point to tell the children exactly what was happening. In the case of some other detainees, their very young children were told that their father had merely gone on vacation. After many years of absence, however, the father might appear to the child to have abandoned the family.

With regard to his relationship with the children and me, before his incarceration, we were lucky if we even had an hour together to discuss things. The only time we had together with the children then would be Sunday. I made it a rule and told him, "Ninoy, basta Sundays sama-sama tayong magsisimba." After mass, we would usually have lunch in a restaurant (oftentimes a Chinese restaurant) or go to a movie. Later on, he also set aside either Holy Week or some other holiday when he would take my children and me to Hong Kong, so we would at least have three days together.

His incarceration, however, allowed us to spend a great deal of quality time together. From Saturday, we would all be there from 11:00 a.m. to 1:00 p.m., at which time the children would leave. I would be with Ninoy from 1:00 p.m. to about 10:00 a.m. the next day, when the children would come for the 11:00 a.m. mass. In that respect, I suppose there would be very few couples that had that amount of quality time. We discussed everything, not just politics; we talked about our children or people we knew, how they had changed or how they were very different from what we originally thought of them.

That was the irony of it all. When Ninoy was in politics, he hardly had time for the family. In fact—and he had written this in his diary—I once chided him for having the time to fly to Jolo at three o'clock in the morning to be a wedding sponsor, but did not have the time to attend his children's affairs. He was so driven to become president then; everything he did was related to achieving this goal.

In prison, he kept praying that God would give him a chance to make it up to all of us. He frequently told us how sorry he was and how guilty he felt that he was hardly around for us, but when his period of crisis came we were all there for him. He told me once, "You know, Cory, I feel so guilty because when I was free and I could do things with our children, I didn't have time for them; and then now they come here every Wednesday, Saturday, and Sunday with no complaints, nothing."

He exerted extra effort to endear himself more to our children. For instance, he would offer to help them with their assignments, telling them, "*O, sige, wala naman akong ginagawa ʻito, ano ang mga* assignment *ninyo?*"

I had brought him sets of both the Encyclopedia Britannica and the American Encyclopedia, and our children seriously took him up on his offer and would ask him to help them. They would tease him about having all the time in his hands and say, "*O*, game, Dad. *Wala ka namang ginagawa ʻito, ʻi ba?*" Of course, he was more than willing to help them with their school work, as he felt he was at least useful in this way.

He very much appreciated our children and promised them that he would make it up to them when his present ordeal was over. He also expressed his hope that we would be able to travel together as a family after all this. Our children would always reassure him and say, "Never mind, Dad, whatever happens . . . " They were simply happy to be with him.

He made a special effort to tell Kris what the situation was because she was only a year-and-a-half old. In fact, Kris actually thought that Ninoy's cell was his home, and each time we would hear rumors that maybe he would be released, Kris would ask, "Mom, *saan titira ang* Daddy?" (Where will Dad live?)

I would say, "*Dito.*" (Here, in the house.)

"*Anong kuwarto niya?*" (Which will be his room?)

"*Ito.*" (This room.)

"Mom, *sa ating ɹalawa ito.*" (This room is ours.)

She couldn't quite understand that, should Ninoy be released from prison, he would be staying in the room she was, for the time being, sharing with me.

At Christmastime, we would be allowed to sleep in his cell on a mattress that we would lay on the cement floor.

One time, Ninoy told me to prepare a bag of toys for Kris and to tell the guard outside to knock on our door at twelve midnight and say that the gifts were from Putris.

When midnight came, the guard knocked on our door and, as instructed, announced, "Package, *po*, for Kris, from Putris!"

Kris asked me, "Mom, *sino si* Putris?" (Who is Putris?)

"*Ay, ewan ko sa* Daddy *mo.*" (Your dad would know.)

Ninoy told her, "*Alam mo, Kris, nakakulong kasi ako kaya* Santa Claus cannot come here. *Ito lang si* Putris *ang nagpapaɹala nitong regalo sa 'yo.*" (You know, Kris, because I'm in prison, Santa Claus cannot come here. Only Putris can send you gifts.)

"Dad, *ako lang ata 'yung merong regalo* from Putris. *'Yung mga kaklase ko at mga kaibigan ko,* from Santa Claus." (I think I'm the only one who receives gifts from Putris. My classmates and friends receive theirs from Santa Claus.)

"*'Di bale. Iba ka, eh.*" (It doesn't matter. You're special.)

Our children grew up exposed to many harsh realities. But this was the period when my family became so much closer. We realized that we just had to stick together, and that no one else could help us but ourselves. For my children, who were aware of what was going on, those were very unusual growing-up or teenage years. I remember Kris telling me how nervous she was at school that particular day because her teacher had asked them to talk about what their fathers did. She said she was glad the teacher was kind enough not to call her. I told her that there was nothing wrong with saying that her dad used to be a senator, but was now a political prisoner. This was nothing to be ashamed of. She told me that no one in her class really knew what a senator was, or what it meant to be a political prisoner. The only thing they knew, she said, was that only bad people went to jail. I reassured her that in time they would understand.

It helped greatly that we were very close as a family. We had only each other to trust, and we could express our fears openly and find comfort in each other. It was this closeness, this bond, which I think, on hindsight, allowed our children to grow up steady and stable during those extraordinary times and to emerge from those painful experiences largely unscathed.

Ninoy also wrote in his diary how grateful he was that he never had to worry about me, where some husbands maybe had to worry and harbor some suspicions. The thought never occurred to him. This was also the time when he started writing poetry, and he wrote at least two long poems for me.

Some of my friends commented on how lucky I was that Ninoy wrote these poems for me. "*Ang suwerte mo naman*, Cory," they told me. "*Sumulat pa ng mga* poems *si* Ninoy."

To which I jokingly remarked, "*Eh, i ipakulong niyo mga asawa niyo para sumulat in ng mga* poems *para sa inyo.*" (Maybe you should send your husbands to jail so that they can also write you poems).

Your will be done, not ours

When Ninoy was transferred back to Fort Bonifacio, he still had an air of disquiet about him. He seemed preoccupied, as if he could not shake off the memories of his ordeal in Fort Magsaysay, the emotional and psychological turmoil it wrought. He never articulated it, but I was made to realize to what extent the experience had almost subdued him when, a month or so after being brought back to Fort Bonifacio, he asked me to reach out to some of our friends who had some links to President Marcos and explore the possibility of putting him instead under house arrest.

I am not anymore sure what transpired exactly, but nothing came of that. The only thing that we could surmise was that many people who were close to Marcos were afraid to be seen as sympathizing with us, lest they be perceived as not being a hundred percent loyal to him.

It was just as well that things happened the way they did because, as the months went by, Ninoy regained his indomitable spirit and resolved to overcome whatever other trials came his way. And, as fate decreed it, Ninoy did have to endure more moments of crisis.

What was going on in Ninoy's mind and heart was something not easily evident or felt by those who did not know him. But I could, in fact, sense the tremendous change not only going on in his mind and heart but also in mine.

He was never a very religious or prayerful person. But when he was sent back to Fort Bonifacio, he was allowed to have only one book, and this was a religious book. Then he was allowed to have a Bible. This, he concentrated on; he read so much of it. I remember Ballsy had to fill out some forms in college and she asked me what to write as her dad's profession. Maybe, I joked, you can put down Vicar of Christ.

He prayed the rosary several times a day, every day. Even while exercising at night in his room, as he walked diagonally from one end to the other, he would pray the rosary. He claimed that there would be days when he would pray it fifty times. He prayed a complete rosary, the three mysteries over and over. He even started writing prayers.

He expressed in a letter to Soc how sorry he was to the Good Lord that, during times of prosperity and fame, he neglected to thank Him for all the blessings showered upon him. And, yet, when he was incarcerated, especially in Fort Magsaysay, he felt so sorry for himself that he would even question God as to why all those terrible things were happening to him.

It was a learning process for him, learning to live in solitude and being shut away from the world when he was such an extrovert. He was really an extrovert with a capital *E*. *Talagang lahat ng tao kailangang kausapin, lahat talaga kailangang puntahan.* (He really felt the need to meet and talk to everyone).

In my case, I love and value my privacy. I was determined to be a good mother and wife, so all my attention was concentrated on bringing up my children well and supporting my husband in his career. I did not have to compete with my husband—that was never my thing. I remember telling Ninoy, "Ninoy, *ikaw naman ang may hilig sa pulitika, bahala ka na 'iyan.*" (When it came to poltics, I left that to him since that was his passion, anyway.)

Of course, I would do some minimal campaigning—shake hands with people in the marketplaces and all—but not give speeches. And, definitely, I never sang! When people would ask me why, I would reply, "*Teka muna, lahat ng halalan na panalo si* Ninoy *'i ako kumanta. Ngayon na kakanta pa ako baka matalo pa 'yan, mabintangan pa ako.*" (In previous elections where

Ninoy won, I never sang. I will not dare sing now as I might be blamed if he loses.)

Before, it was as if he knew it all. Nobody could tell him what to do or what not to do, and it was very rare when he would ask me for any advice. But since he was in prison and was locked up, he needed to rely on us.

Prior to his imprisonment, I never talked with Ninoy's fellow politicians or fellow senators because it was really not my thing, and I was wary that I might make mistakes. Besides, they were not asking for my opinion. But, at the same time, given our situation then, they also had few choices. They would tell me, "Cory, *pag nakita mo si* Ninoy, *pakitanong mo lamang ito.*" (Cory, can you please ask Ninoy about this when you see him.) So, of course, I would try to remember all of their messages and, when I would see Ninoy, I would relay to him their questions. After he would tell me what to tell them, I would get back to them and give them the answer.

I also needed to attend the meetings of Ninoy's lawyers. They would explain to me what they were trying to do and, of course, they would always tell me that we had no chance. "This is martial law," they would say, "and only one man makes the laws. And, even if we have the best arguments, we will never win." It was as if they wanted me to fix deep in my mind that it was a no-win situation and not give me the false notion that there was a chance of victory here.

Then there were the requests for interviews I needed to accommodate. I would tell him, "You know, Ninoy, I have to give interviews now to foreign media and I really don't feel up to it." He would then reassure me, "No, no, no, don't worry. I'll help you." So, he would make up all these questions and then he would tell me how best to answer them.

I would tell him, "My gosh. Okay, it's bad enough you're in jail, but now I have to do all of these things." I suppose, however, when you don't have a choice you just need to learn and try to do the best you can. I also have Sen. Jovy Salonga to thank because, the first few times that I would give a press conference, I would request him to be present so that, should he notice that I am having difficulty answering some questions, he can save me and maybe help me answer them. I did have a lot of help and in time, I guess, my confidence did build up.

I also detected a change in the way people regarded us during those times. Before martial law, I remember I was shopping in Unimart once and there came this woman running from across the other side calling out to me. She told me, "*Huwag mo akong kalimutan pag* president *na si* Ninoy." (I hope you don't forget me when Ninoy becomes president.)

After, when martial law happened, I remember I was in church and *parang walang nakakita sa iyo.* (It was as if I was invisible to the people.)

When Ninoy found out someone we knew died, he asked me if I had gone to the wake. I told him, "*Alam mo,* Ninoy, *iba na ngayon, eh. Baka matakot pa 'yung pamilya ng namatay. Dahil kung pupunta ako ʹoon, baka ma-*black list *pa sila.*" I did not want the family of the deceased to feel anxious by my presence there, as they might be black-listed by the government. Still, he insisted that I go, and I remember saying, "No, Ninoy. I'm telling you. You don't know what it's like on the outside."

Once, he forced me to go to a wedding and so I went with my sister-in-law, Maur. True enough, *walang tumabi sa amin sa* table. No one sat with us. But, at that point, you don't really care anymore. And then you just tell yourself, "Oh, well, that's how life is."

So it was, from being so public a figure, Ninoy became a private, isolated person, forced to be by himself, meditating and writing. I, on the other hand, from being someone who preferred a private life, suddenly had to take care of everything outside of the children and the home, like deal with the military and foreign correspondents. Looking back, however, I somehow believe that the trials we had to go through during the time of martial law brought out the best in Ninoy and me—not that I want to thank President Marcos for it!

Ninoy would sometimes say, "*Sana sinabi na lang* from the beginning,

'Okay, Ninoy, you will stay in prison for seven years, seven months, and so many days.' Then, every day, I could look at my calendar and say, '*O, sige, ilan na lamang.*'" There was never anything like that, so that he could not tell how many days he had left.

If Ninoy had gone through just a short detention, maybe he would not have become the person that he became. There were so many others who were arrested and detained and, of course, they suffered also. But, as time passed, they seemed to have forgotten what they had experienced. In Ninoy's case, I think it really grew roots; he learned very much from that very difficult experience. And so did I.

In the beginning, we were both complaining. Why is this happening to us? We're not saints, but definitely we're not the big sinners that other people are. And yet they are free to do their own thing, while here we are having to suffer all these trials.

I remember one of my nun friends told me then, "You know, Cory, Jesus only sends sufferings to those whom he loves."

And I said, "Oh, Sister, I hope he doesn't love me too much so there won't be too many sufferings." Of course, I said it as a joke. Still I felt, okay, thank you for loving me, but maybe not so much.

So it took, I would say, almost a year and a half or close to two, when we finally accepted the fact that, yes, maybe we have not sinned as badly or have not been as terrible as other people, but let us think of Jesus Christ who certainly did not do wrong and yet He had to suffer and die for our sins. Little by little, I guess we were accepting the fact that, yes, this is how it is.

The best thing that happened to both of us was we really became very much closer to the Lord. We held to our belief that, whatever happens, the best thing to do is to just entrust yourself and all your problems to the Lord.

Fake news in the 1970s

Ninoy had been in detention for eleven months without having any charges filed against him in all that time. It was only eleven months after his arrest in September 1972 that he was brought to face the military court and charges of subversion and illegal possession of firearms were filed against him. An additional charge of murder was also eventually brought against him.

In those first eleven months, we were aware that a number of our close associates and the people who worked for Ninoy had also been arrested and detained.

One of our drivers, in fact, was first to be arrested and detained. He had a photograph of Ninoy and the military authorities ordered him to eat it. They told him, "*Ayan 'yung amo mo; kainin mo 'yung letrato.*" His wife, one of the *yayas* of my children who later on served as my cook, was also picked up and detained. She was three months pregnant then, and was threatened that if she did not cooperate she would be kept in Crame until after she gave birth to her child. They questioned her about Ninoy's visitors to the house, asking her what they talked about. In reply, she said that there were so many people who came to visit and that, since she was only a maid, she never sat in on any of the conversations. (It made us wonder who these people questioning them were.)

Our other driver actually suffered worse. They beat him up so badly. They placed a briefcase on the side of his head and jumped on it so that his hearing was permanently impaired.

The military had arrested so many people. Even his official photographer was arrested! When Ninoy discovered the extent of these arrests, he instructed me to tell these people to go ahead and confess whatever it was they were being forced to confess, to sign whatever statement they were being forced to sign. He felt it unfair that innocent people be made to suffer alongside him. In any case, Ninoy believed it was a "kangaroo" court, anyway, so there was nothing to it.

It was not enough that they had jailed Ninoy. They also made sure that they had many witnesses to testify against him. The situation posed a dilemma for many, and it was especially difficult for those people who worked with Ninoy, who felt that they were being disloyal to him. But Ninoy told me to assure them that, knowing the circumstances, he would understand. Until I told them it was all right to sign those so-called confessions, they probably would still have held out and waited. There were some, of course, who needed no urging to sign, who did so willingly, and who proved to be such disappointments in this way.

The military captured some of the leading members of the New People's Army (NPA) as well. These were the people the military used to testify against Ninoy. Commander Melody became a state witness, and Ninoy pointed out that, under normal times, the state witness is also a co-accused, but one who is least guilty. In the case of Commander Melody, he had confessed to killing many members of the PC and many civilians alike.

Afterwards, these people were eliminated. Commander Melody was gunned down in Nepo Mart, in Angeles, Pampanga. Another member of the NPA also died under very mysterious circumstances. The Marcos dictatorship wanted to impute that these witnesses were killed on orders of Ninoy. It seemed like every imaginable crime was being imputed to Ninoy.

Ninoy, at first, was willing to participate in the trial, but the murder charge only came later. Ninoy then felt that these people were just wanting to demolish him, and ridicule him, and make him a non-entity insofar as the Filipinos were concerned. Ninoy's argument was also that, being a civilian, he should be brought before a civil court. At that time, the civil courts were still operating. Martial law had not abolished them.

He spoke with his lawyers, Senator Tañada and Jovy. Senator Tañada told Ninoy that, if he did not recognize the jurisdiction of the military commission over him, then all he had to do was announce his intent that he would not participate. Jovy, on the other hand, thought that Ninoy should participate in the trial. He told me that, even if Marcos had everything under his control and the military commission was simply going to obey him and follow his directions to the letter, why not buy time. If Ninoy participated, it would give the defense a chance to bring on their own witnesses and to cross-examine the prosecution's witnesses as well. His point was that, by participating, we could buy time, that as the trial dragged on we might see the end of martial law and Ninoy could have his day in court.

Senator Tañada and Jovy explained to me what I should expect during the trial. Senator Tañada said that the fact that Ninoy would not participate and would announce that he did not recognize the authority of the military court over him, a civilian, in all likelihood the prosecution would merely enumerate the charges against him and not even bother to bring on any witnesses, since Ninoy was not going to refute them anyway. Senator Tañada also warned me to prepare for the possibility that, on the first day of the trial, it could all be over, that Ninoy could right there and then be sentenced to death by firing squad. The charges against Ninoy were of crimes that entailed the heaviest penalty.

The first military commission trial was set for August 1973. For this first trial, I asked the family pediatrician to prescribe some medication for the children to calm them, just a mild dose, because I was sure they were going to be crying. I forget now what she prescribed, but whatever it was had the opposite effect on my second daughter Pinky. She was crying uncontrollably from beginning to end and, afterwards, lost both her contact lenses without her even realizing it! At a certain point, Pinky was talking to Kris and Kris told her, "Pinky, *baka pukpukin ang ulo natin ng* general." (The general might hit us on the head.) Gen. Jose Syjuco had been banging away with his gavel and had said that he would send out anyone he caught talking or laughing or smiling.

I remember these humorous incidents now, but it was then a very grave situation.

A forty-day hunger strike
and a death wish

In 1975, Ninoy was again called to face charges in the military court. And, as in 1973, he refused to participate once more. It was at this time, on April 4, when Ninoy declared that he would go on a hunger strike. Fr. Horacio dela Costa had, I think, previously been able to visit him twice, and they had discussed his going on this hunger strike, which as it turned out would stretch to forty days.

On the first day of his hunger strike, I brought a cheese sandwich. Ninoy said that he could smell the cheese, and so I had to step outside to eat it. A tuna fish sandwich was obviously impossible. At the same time, I had to eat also. It couldn't be the two of us fasting.

Aside from me, an aide from the Fort Bonifacio hospital had been assigned to stay the night with Ninoy, in case something happened to him. We worried then that the clippings and Xeroxed copies we had smuggled in would be discovered, so we decided to burn these in the bathroom. Of course, we didn't know that, when burned, these Xeroxed copies would give off a very bad smell. And the bathroom was so smoky!

In the beginning of his hunger strike, Ninoy would get dizzy often and sleep most of the day. Later, as the hunger strike progressed, he could not sleep for long periods. He would sleep then waken, but not be fully in control, not fully understand what was happening because he was just too weak. It was just so frightening. I myself was losing a lot of weight.

At first, I was allowed to visit him every day so I could supervise him, because what he needed to do every day was to take a bath. To aid him, I had to position three folding chairs between his bed and the bathroom so that he could rest as he slowly made his way to his bath. I would pour the water over his head, which brought him relief. He had these shivers and would be cold all the time, so I would place socks on his feet and make sure the air-conditioner was always turned off. Ninoy was also emitting this foul odor. Apparently, when a person is on a hunger strike, he emits a foul odor as he burns his ketones. This happens when the person begins to burn the fat, and then the muscles, in his body. We thought the odor was coming from the mouth, so even Senator Tañada and Soc, who had visited Ninoy, told me to send him mouthwash. But the odor was actually coming from the pores.

During this time I kept telling Ninoy, "I hope you will not have a death wish and just surrender to the Lord and do whatever it is that He wants of you. But don't go. There's still so much that we have to do."

Ninoy's response to me was, "You know, if I go, then my suffering will end and that is my prayer. But, if I don't go, then that means Jesus wants me to do something more."

I encouraged him to think of it that way. I did not want him contemplating a death wish.

On the thirtieth day of Ninoy's hunger strike, Cardinal Sin came with Bishop Gabby Reyes (he was the assistant then, not yet a bishop) to give Ninoy the anointing of the sick. He was told, though, that the host he was going to give Ninoy had to be examined. They could not even give him any communion. That being the case, Cardinal Sin decided that we would receive the host ourselves.

While Cardinal Sin administered the sacrament and was praying over him, Ninoy's tears just kept flowing. It was a very moving experience. Later on, I asked Ninoy how he felt and he said he felt that he had made peace with the Lord and that he was prepared to go. I had to tell him again, "No. Don't think of it that way."

On the thirty-fifth day of his hunger strike, when I arrived for my visit in Fort Bonifacio, I was told that something terrible had happened. Ninoy had collapsed and had to be rushed to the Intensive Care Unit (ICU) of Veterans Memorial Hospital. I thought that he had died. When I got to the hospital, much to my relief, he was sleeping. I learned later that the military doctors had wanted to give him dextrose intravenously. But Ninoy insisted that he drink it. This was fortunate because, as the doctors in Veterans told him (and, later on, his doctors in Dallas when we went for his surgery), if he had taken it intravenously, the nutrients would merely go to his veins and not to his intestines. Taking the dextrose orally prevented his intestines from adhering.

All throughout Ninoy's hunger strike, nightly masses were being said for him in Greenhills, and shuttling from the hospital to the church and back became my routine.

I also sought the advice of Father dela Costa, Bishop Francisco Claver, and Fr. Frederik Fermin, a theologian from the University of Santo Tomas, on what I could tell Ninoy to convince him to end his hunger strike. It was also important to me that I be able to explain to other people, from a theologian's point of view, that what Ninoy was doing was not a form of suicide.

Bishop Claver wrote Ninoy a note, which I hid under the arch of my foot. (I preferred to wear open-toed shoes; otherwise, during searches, the military authorities would always ask me to remove my shoes. This way, they did not need to.) It was difficult to walk, but I managed to bring the note in to Ninoy. Bishop Claver told me to explain to Ninoy that even if it seemed that what he was fasting and praying for had not been granted, it did not mean that God did not appreciate his sacrifice. It only meant, perhaps, that God felt this was not the right time to grant it. Father dela Costa also conveyed the message to Ninoy, through me, that he agreed to the fast only because he thought it was going to be for a limited time. His understanding was that it would not be until death.

There was another group—Fr. Toti Olaguer, Soc, and others—who felt that Ninoy should go on with the hunger strike. Others were saying he shouldn't, because, if he died, what would happen? I think it was just through the intercession of Our Lady of Fatima that this crisis was resolved.

On the fortieth day of his hunger strike, Ninoy told me that he was feeling the urge to go to the bathroom. I was wondering how that could be when he had not been eating anything in the last forty days. Ninoy thought it was probably the capsules, the medicines (potassium, amino acids, and others) prescribed to him, that he needed to expel. While in the bathroom, he began to feel dizzy. (Apparently, forceful straining or painful retching can cause a reflex that can lower the heart rate and blood pressure, which in turn can cause a heart attack in an already compromised heart. The pulse rate becomes so low and, when people strain, it becomes even lower. This is what doctors usually recommend to their patients, that when their pulse rate is high, they should go to the bathroom and strain to bring the pulse rate down.) I called out to the guards to help me carry Ninoy back to his bed. The doctors were summoned, and they told him that they wanted to do some tests. As Ninoy kept nodding his head, I thought all the while that he was well aware of what was happening.

Hearing of the incident, my mother-in-law hurried to the hospital and appealed to Ninoy to put an end to his hunger strike. I, on my part, assured him that he had already successfully proven his point. To persuade him further, I told him that friends who knew people in the military had heard that Marcos would not allow him to die, but that Marcos also would not do anything to prevent him from lapsing into a coma and becoming a vegetable. What good to the country would he be then?

Finally, we were able to prevail upon him to put an end to his hunger strike. That day happened to be the day of the Feast of Our Lady of Fatima.

Slowly, Ninoy worked to regain his strength. Like a baby, he started by being fed two tablespoons of rice cereal every two hours.

Then, as if I needed any more trials, something happened again.

I like to do gardening. I like plants. One day, Kris followed me out into the garden. Ninoy's two dogs, Weimaraners named Meldy and Ferdie, also happened to be there. They were used to seeing me, but I guess when they saw Kris embracing me, they thought that Kris was hurting me. The dogs grabbed onto her with their jaws and would not let go. I found myself on my knees holding Kris and shouting, "Meldy! Ferdie!" My neighbors must have thought that I had gone crazy!

The whole episode lasted no more than a minute. We rushed Kris to the Far Eastern University Hospital where she underwent surgery. If the dogs had gotten to her main artery, it would have been the end. I told my other children to go and visit their dad in the hospital, and tell him that I had a headache so I couldn't come. It was only the next day that I got to tell Ninoy what happened.

It was at this time that Maur telephoned Father Fermin so I could speak to him. I lamented to him that I did not know what it was that I had done to have all these terrible things happening to me. I thought, what could possibly happen next? I felt like Job! I was feeling so helpless and ready to give up. Father Fermin consoled me by saying that this was just a time of great testing.

The Dictator and other prison mates

In all those years that Ninoy was in prison, only once did he come face to face with Marcos. This was sometime in 1976, after the hunger strike, when Ninoy was brought to Malacañang. Ninoy and Marcos were "brods," since they both belonged to the Upsilon Sigma Phi fraternity, and even addressed each other as such.

Marcos engaged Ninoy in small talk at first, asking if he had enough books. Ninoy told him that he did, and that they had also allowed him to have a TV. Then Marcos commented that he envied Ninoy all that time he had available to read. To this, Ninoy replied that he would still gladly change places with Marcos, even for a day.

I suppose it was all part of psychological warfare when Marcos told Ninoy that he felt bad because all Ninoy's friends and allies were turning against him. He said that Commander Dante, an NPA leader who had been recently captured, was planning to testify against Ninoy and say that they had been meeting. But Ninoy told Marcos that there was no need for sympathy because, if Marcos were in his place, Ninoy felt sure that even his own brother-in-law, Kokoy Romualdez, would testify against him, too.

Marcos also asked him what he would do if he were released. Ninoy answered that he would go out into the streets and inquire of the people if they were content with Marcos, with martial law. And if they told him they were, then he would keep his peace. But if they were not, then he would continue to oppose Marcos.

We never uncovered what Marcos's reason was for calling Ninoy to

Malacañang, although Ninoy had earlier expressed a wish to meet with him. (He had also wanted to meet with Eddie Ramos, but he never got to do so.) Perhaps Marcos wanted to see what Ninoy's frame of mind was, to see if he was already willing to give up the struggle, to make a deal, as in the case of others who had been incarcerated, like Nilo Tayag had done. Luis Taruc had also become very supportive of Marcos.

Maybe Marcos wanted to impress upon Ninoy that there were very few of them on Ninoy's side left, and that it was pointless to continue to make life miserable for himself. Whatever the purpose of this meeting was, it only convinced Ninoy more than ever that he should remain where he was—in prison—where he would continue his fight.

Because Ninoy endured many years of detention, our family life was quite unconventional. In spite of this, however, we tried to make things as normal as possible. And, this, we were able to do with the support of other people as well.

Ninoy never really cared for alcohol. Then suddenly he craved for wine, Sauternes, I think it was. (I am not sure what brought this on. Maybe because it was a forbidden thing. Maybe he just wanted to get back at his jailers, to get one over them.) I tested to see which soft drink it resembled most in color, whether it was Coke or Pepsi. Because the color was most similar to Pepsi, I called up my brother-in-law, Baby, whose company, MANLO, used to make crown caps for Pepsi. I told him of my plan to send wine to Ninoy and Baby reassured me that it would be no problem because they had the machine to put on the caps.

We ate with Ninoy on Sundays, and we would usually bring a case of Pepsi. One bottle of wine could fill three bottles of Pepsi, and so I mixed in these three bottles filled with wine with the other soft drink bottles in the case.

In Ninoy's room, I saw that the food I brought was already there. However, the case of Pepsi was not. Ninoy asked where it had gone and, much later, a soldier came and told us that there had been a mistake. The case of Pepsi had been loaded into some officer's car, but he told us not to worry because they would replace it! Eventually, they found it, and I pointed out to Ninoy the three bottles filled with wine. These were the ones with the cleanest and shiniest crown caps.

Ninoy was also fond of dogs (though I was not), and when my niece, Gina, the eldest daughter of Baby and Terry, told us that her dog, Dollars, had had puppies, we decided to ask for one. I told Noynoy to carry the puppy in and, if anybody asked, to simply say that we wanted to show it to Ninoy. If nobody asked, then he could leave the dog inside. It was a Japanese Spitz, and Ninoy named her Mako.

This dog was very different from other dogs. For one thing, she did not know how to bark. For another, she liked Pepsi, mint candy, and chocolates. (It was a good thing the dog did not turn out diabetic!) She could also perform tricks, like begging. Ninoy really loved that dog. It cheered him, I think, that at least he had some other warm, breathing, living thing with which he could interact in one way or another within the confines of his cell.

Inevitably, Mako matured and went on heat, so we decided to bring her out of Fort Bonifacio, find her a mate, and bring her back. When the time came, Mako had her litter—right there on Ninoy's bed! There was blood all over. Ninoy knocked on his door (we called it a tabernacle door because it had a smaller door on the top part, which the guards could open from the outside) to ask the guard for help. The guard, in turn, went to get someone else. In the meantime, Ninoy in his cell was picking up the puppies one by one with Kleenex tissues.

Of course, I had to bring Mako and all these puppies out and deal with giving them all away.

Once, we brought Ninoy an aquarium, but he overfed the fish and they all died. I suppose it was for lack of anything to do, so he kept feeding the fish. Cecile Mitra, Monching's wife, also gifted him with a bird. It was supposed to be a talking bird, but it never talked.

I remember also that there was this little mouse inside his room. Ninoy insisted that I leave it alone. It was the only living thing with him in the room, and didn't I read about the saints and all that? I had to remind him that the floor was where we slept when I was allowed to stay over. So I told him, it was either the mouse or me. Finally, Ninoy relented and I brought some sticky fly paper to catch the mouse.

Courage, like cowardice, is infectious

His years in detention, plus total government control of the media during martial law, had almost succeeded in reducing Ninoy to an insignificant figure in the political scene. He was slipping into oblivion. And apart from the old opposition stalwarts, his family and friends, the rest of the population knew little or nothing about him.

Ninoy's faith in the Filipino people was, however, unwavering. I always used to tell him that the Filipinos were different now, more scared, and fearful. But Ninoy never experienced any of this cowardice that we were naturally exposed to, so he was very forgiving of the Filipino people. He always used to say that courage, like cowardice, is infectious. And that all it needs is for one man to show the way and the others will follow. He would say that it was only because they had no leader. All that was needed was for one person to go out there and rally the people. He kept telling me not to lose hope.

When Marcos called for the Batasang Pambansa elections in 1978, the Liberal Party (LP) at first planned to participate until Marcos decided that the elections would be through block voting. Gerry, Jovy, and other leaders of the LP strongly felt that their chance of winning would be next to none if the elections were through block voting. The whole exercise was a farce, a joke at their expense. So they decided to boycott the elections, and of course Ninoy had to go along with that decision.

Then Charito Planas came to see me and asked if Ninoy would like to lead a ticket. Senator Tañada encouraged this, as it would provide the opposition with a forum, an opportunity to reach out to the people. Ninoy asked me to ask Gerry and the others if they could grant him this chance. It would allow him to connect with people and let them know that he was still alive. And if he won, who knows, he might be able to regain his freedom.

We began raising money for the campaign, with Ninoy surreptitiously sending out notes and messages again through us. I had asked Ninoy to write everything down because I was hesitant and didn't want to say outright that we were asking for contributions. I would then give these notes to the would-be contributors, whom I would meet with at night. You can just imagine how scared everyone was at that time.

Eventually, we were able to field a slate of twenty-one candidates under the Lakas ng Bayan (LABAN) party, and it was quite a mix. We had among them, Alex Boncayao, Trining Herrera, Charito Planas, and Gerry Barican, who at that time were considered radical. Tito Guingona was the last to join up. He could not come to a decision at first, until that very day when I was scheduled to give a press conference to announce the twenty-one.

Our hopes were high. Even if, in the beginning, there would hardly be any people attending our rallies, we were assured that, at the very least, the families of the twenty-one candidates would be there. We knew, however, that the people were listening. From behind open windows, from inside their houses, they were listening. They were just so afraid.

It was during this LABAN campaign that we discovered Kris's penchant for public speaking. One of the local journalists, Doy del Castillo, had got to talking to Kris and he asked me, "*Gusto niyo ho turuan ko magtalumpati si Kris?*" He had mentioned that his father had also been imprisoned before and I guess this gesture—his offering to coach Kris on public speaking— was his way of sympathizing with us.

As it happened, Pinky, who was a member of the Economics Society of the University of the Philippines (UP), had been asked to speak for the LABAN campaign. She in turn asked Kris if she wanted to speak in her place and promised her a prize if she did. And, Kris, all of seven years old, said yes. I did not go with them to UP because I was afraid Kris would act up if she saw me. Before she left, Kris was all excited and eager to go. Once in UP, however, Kris all of a sudden declared that she was not going to speak. And when Pinky asked her why, Kris said, *"Bakit ako lang ang walang sampaguita* lei?" She had noticed that all the other speakers had a *sampaguita* lei, except her. So Charito Planas gave hers to Kris, and everything went smoothly afterwards.

Kris was an impressive speaker—giving seventeen speeches in all—and the people responded well to her.

At that time, Imelda commented to her friends privately, although it reached us, that these Aquinos took advantage of their children. Well, we thought, this could easily be remedied if she only allowed Ninoy to speak. After aiming this pointed criticism at us, she then invited Niño Muhlach to the Kilusan ng Bagong Lipunan (KBL) rallies. Sure, he was a movie star. But his father was not a candidate and neither was he in jail, so the people could not relate to him emotionally. He did not click as well.

It was also during this campaign when Ninoy was given that one interview in the TV program *Face the Nation*. Initially, I was not in favor of it, and told him so. I felt that he would be taking such a risk because all the TV stations were under the control of the dictator and they could cast him in a negative light. But Ninoy was encouraged because Lupita assured him that she would be around during the actual taping of the show. They had also come to an agreement that if either side backed out, the show would not be aired.

This was one instance when I was glad Ninoy followed his instincts. As it turned out, it was the best performance of his life. And that night, it was in fact noted that there were very few cars out on the streets. It seemed that everyone was glued to their TV sets and was very much interested in seeing, and listening to, him. More than anything else, it set to rest all the nasty talk about him having gone crazy. That was the talk before, and people could very well believe how someone could really go crazy given the very terrible situation Ninoy was in.

His appearance on TV also had a very important influence on the campaign. In the beginning, as I said, and out of fear, only very few people would attend our rallies and these were mostly limited to the candidates' families. But after the *Face the Nation* program, people not only became more interested in what the LABAN candidates were doing, but were emboldened to attend our rallies as well. We were able to draw bigger and bigger crowds as the campaign progressed, but did not realize how great an impact Ninoy's appearance had on it until its memorable finale—the noise barrage—took place.

Ballsy had received a chain letter at the office where she was working at the time. The letter urged people to make noise through however way they could—be it by banging on pots and pans or blowing their car horns—wherever they would be at a certain time and date. This was to signify to Marcos, in an unmistakably clear and audible way, the people's support for Ninoy and the other LABAN candidates.

I smuggled this letter in to Ninoy, and he instructed us to support this effort. We made more copies of the letter and distributed them and, on April 6, 1978, the scheduled day of the noise barrage, we gave a press conference. The foreign correspondents present there were asking where this noise barrage was going to be held. I told them that I honestly could not tell them where, specifically. People were just too frightened to give us any inkling of what they were going to do.

The noise barrage was supposed to start at nine o'clock in the evening. A little before nine, I told my children and all our househelp to go out on the street in front of our house and start making noise so our neighbors would be a little encouraged. As it turned out, encouragement was unnecessary. The noise was completely deafening and seemed to go on and on, endlessly! We called people to find out how it was in their areas and everywhere it was the same report—loud and long.

The ironic thing however was, Ninoy, who was supposed to be the beneficiary of this noise barrage, heard not a thing from where he was. In his cell in Fort Bonifacio, he was isolated and too far away.

While it was exhilarating and encouraging for all of us, this show of support for the opposition was in fact what led Marcos to decide to make it a 21-0 victory in favor of the KBL. It was probably the first time anyone had any sense of what the opposition was all about. During the campaign, there had been no letters to the editor, no big rallies, but just, at most, only ten thousand people in attendance. Nothing as big and "deafening" as this, with the sounds of protest reverberating throughout Metro Manila. But Marcos took it as a cue that no way would he let anybody in the opposition win.

The next morning, when we were voting, the cheating began. Noynoy reported to me that they were pushed out of the precinct to which he was assigned. Then, when I went around Makati with Lupita and Tessie, we saw in one of the schools the teachers themselves stuffing the ballot boxes. I asked one of the teachers why she was doing that, and she answered, "Bakit, sino ka ba?" (Why, who are you, anyway?)

I told her who I was, that I was the wife of a candidate. Lupita suggested that we take pictures, just to scare her. Later on, my lawyers told me that I was not entitled to go to a precinct unless I was named a watcher. We went to other places, like Malabon, where we saw people walking around with Armalites. I felt that nothing was going to come of these elections.

I had been scheduled to give a press conference at five that afternoon, but I asked for an hour's delay as I was feeling downhearted and dejected. At the press conference, I was supposed to say that, contrary to what Marcos claimed, we had scored a moral victory. My thought at that time however was, as the cliché goes, there's no substitute for real victory.

We visited Ninoy on the Sunday after the elections. I told him that we had done enough, that we had done our best under the circumstances. I made him promise me one thing, that, if ever he would run for office again, he should wait until he was out of jail. I did not feel like going through the whole thing again, asking for contributions, strategizing, and campaigning. Little did I know that, years later, I would have to do it for myself!

That Sunday, protest actions against the electoral fraud had been scheduled, with one group congregating at the Manila Cathedral and the other marching to the cathedral from Santo Domingo Church.

We were waiting for our car after our visit to Ninoy, but it never came, so we decided instead to walk to the guard post. On our way there, a jeepney passed and the driver stopped for us. We got in and the driver asked where we came from. I told him that we had just come from visiting Ninoy and, when he found out who my husband was, he reported to us that the marchers from Santo Domingo had been arrested and brought to Bicutan. Among them were Senator Tañada, Soc, and Tito Guingona. I think this was Soc and Tito's second arrest. Immediately I thought of Noynoy, who had joined the protesters at the cathedral. That was all I needed, I thought, a husband in jail, and now a son! Fortunately it did not come to that, as he had been able to leave the cathedral when news of the arrests came.

As I felt I was already a veteran of such things, I volunteered to be the spokesperson of the wives of those who had been arrested. I also volunteered to accompany them to see Eddie Ramos, chief of the PC that was in charge of Bicutan. Eddie says he does not remember this. But I did go see him, together with Mrs. Tañada, Bing Pimentel (wife of Nene Pimentel) Ruth Guingona (who even bravely insisted to also be detained), and others, to ask him to allow them to see their husbands.

The living conditions in Bicutan were lamentable, to say the least. For one thing, they had no proper toilets, just a hole in the ground in each cell. People were also saying that Senator Tañada should be set free in deference to his age. Eventually, due in part to the adverse worldwide publicity sparked by these arrests, they were released.

CHAPTER II
Exile & Assassination
1979 – 1983

A heart attack and a new lease on life

There had been talk for some time that Ninoy was soon going to be released, and in June 1979, we were called to discuss this possibility. We were very happy to hear this! Senator Tañada was present at this meeting, while Enrile and now-general Josephus Ramas (formerly colonel) represented the government. They told us that they had heard talk that Ninoy would be allowed to leave the country on the condition that he make a solemn pledge not to say anything that would be inimical to the interests of the government. Ninoy, who felt that the interests of the government were different from the interests of the country, suggested that "government" be changed to "country." Of course, they would not allow this. I said I hoped we would be allowed to come back since my eldest daughter was planning to get married. They told me that perhaps I would be allowed to come back, but Ninoy would not be allowed to do so.

Ninoy began packing his things—all his books, too, including the volumes of Encyclopedia Britannica and American Encyclopedia that I had gotten for him—and had them brought out. Then we waited. June passed without any word from the government, then July, then August. Still nothing! Finally, Ninoy told us to just bring his things back.

Then, suddenly, on December 22, while I was visiting Ninoy, someone came for him and told him that General Ramas wanted to talk to him. I think Gen. Fabian Ver had also arrived there.

I watched some videos while waiting (televisions and Betamax machines were allowed, but not radios), and I had already watched a number of them when Ninoy came back with the news that they were letting us go home.

This Christmas furlough in 1979 was his second time home. The first was when the authorities had allowed him to come home overnight for our silver wedding anniversary on October 11. But of course, that time, he did not sleep! He was so excited to be back home that he stayed awake for thirty-six hours. He felt that he could sleep all he wanted in Fort Bonifacio, anyway. But when would he have the chance to see or talk to all these people again?

When we got home that December of 1979, all the children were so surprised! Once home, we called our relatives and friends, and soon people began coming to the house non-stop. All those eighteen days that Ninoy was home, there was just a constant stream of people at all times of the day and night, as some even came at midnight. It was all talk, talk, talk!

This homecoming also became for me a ceaseless round of preparing food and drinks, to the extent that I told the help not to remove the place settings on the tables anymore. I felt like I was running a *carinieria* (Filipino fast food restaurant)! Much as I wanted to spend more time with Ninoy while he was home, there came a point when I felt so exhausted that I locked myself in Ballsy's room. I just wanted to rest. I could hear people looking for me, but I pretended not to hear. I was ready to collapse!

Then on March 19, 1980, Ninoy suffered a heart attack. He had these terrible chest pains as if, as he described it to us when we visited him, a carabao were sitting on his chest. The doctors in Fort Bonifacio had examined him and told him that it might have been just a muscle spasm because he was exercising too much.

Dr. Pepot San Gabriel also came to Fort Bonifacio to examine him. But without the proper facilities, how thorough or accurate can the examination be, what kind of checking could they do there? They took Ninoy's blood pressure and conducted an electro-cardiogram (ECG) test. His health continued to deteriorate. I remember confiding this to Soc, and he advised me to keep this secret because the opposition might get demoralized. I myself was thinking that at least while he was strong and healthy, there was still hope, that we could still spend time together and as a family. Faced with Ninoy's illness, I felt like all could be lost.

The authorities finally decided to transfer him to the Philippine Heart Center for tests. The day before he was to be brought there, the doctor who was in charge of him, Colonel Garcia, came and told him that arrangements were being made for the transfer. While the doctor was making his phone calls, he himself suffers a heart attack, and dies. The doctor, who was supposed to be looking after Ninoy, dies. He dies on Ninoy's desk! It was one of life's morbid turn of events, tragic and also very surreal.

Ninoy from the start declared that he would much rather die in Fort Bonifacio than be operated on at the Heart Center. This he made clear to Undersec. Mike Barbero, when he came to talk to Ninoy. He suggested that Ninoy write a flattering letter to Imelda, which he did, profuse with thanks and praise. This is the reason for that picture with the message, "Thank you very much for this hospital, which I criticized in the past . . ."

While the doctors were preparing to conduct tests on him, Ninoy suffered another heart attack. As the incident was recorded, the doctors told him that now they were very sure he had some blockages. Angiogram would have to be done and possibly surgery. Ninoy had instructed me to call Dr. Rolly Solis, our family friend, in the US to ask him what should be done. Rolly told me to tell Ninoy not to have the angiogram done here. At that time, one could die from an angiogram. Besides, in the beginning, the Heart Center had many casualties.

On May 8, Ninoy observed that someone important might be coming because the guards were all dressed in *barong* and people were cleaning the hospital with such meticulous care. And true enough, lo and behold, there was Imelda, a vision in a pink *terno*, walking in with Mel Mathay. She told Ninoy that she was sorry to see him looking so poorly. Ninoy, in reply, could not help saying that he was that way because of her.

Then Imelda proceeded to hold forth on her ideologies, complete with diagrams, even. After she finished, she asked Ninoy, quite suddenly, if he wanted to leave that night on a Philippine Airlines flight to the US. Of course, Ninoy immediately said yes! And just like that, Imelda telephoned General Ver to help us with our passports and visas.

I remember that Mel Mathay called again to confirm with me when I wanted to leave. When I told him we could leave the next day, Ninoy, however, reminded me that to delay our leaving might give them time to change their minds, so it would be best if I went along with the plans.

I had a million and one things to do! I had to go to the embassy to get our visas. Ninoy's passport was not even laminated or signed. I had to go to the bank. I had to sign my powers of attorney, because I did not know when we would be coming back. I gave my sister, Terry, money for the maids and told her to see to the house. Everything was done in such a rush!

By the time I got home, a number of people were already gathered there. My friends Reggie Coseteng and Connie Lopez volunteered to pack for me so I had no way of knowing what was in my suitcase. It was only when we got to San Francisco that I saw that they had even packed a statue of the Sacred Heart!

Imelda had told Ninoy that she would send a doctor to accompany us. He was a young doctor, who I imagined was just a resident. Sometime during the flight, Ninoy again felt ill. I asked the doctor what to do, but he seemed not to know, asking if things were not explained to us before we left. I ended up having to read the doctor's instructions myself and deciding which medicine in the list Ninoy could take. So Ninoy took this medicine and, fortunately, soon felt better. And, when a stewardess came and asked him what he would like to have, Ninoy said, "Everything!" He had not had such a variety of food in a while, but of course he could hardly eat from all the excitement.

We had been told that we could bring only three of our five children. This was, I suppose, a form of guarantee. What they did not know, however, was that two of them were already out of the country. Viel was in the US and Pinky was in Hong Kong working for IBM.

Pinky, in fact, was unaware of all the recent events until she turned on the TV and heard on the news that Senator Aquino had had a heart attack, was given only six months to live, and had left the country to go to the US. This was shocking news for her, and all she could do was cry and cry. Not only because she was worried about her dad, but also because she thought that we had completely forgotten about her and had abandoned her! It was just that we could not call her from Manila because the phone lines were bugged.

Eventually, she was able to get in touch with my sister, Terry, who reassured her that we would call her from San Francisco and also that her dad was fine. When we got to San Francisco, we called her and asked if she had enough money, or if she knew someone she could borrow money from, for a plane ticket to the US. Since she did not want to borrow a large sum, she decided to buy just a one-way ticket to San Francisco. Of course, she was questioned about it by the US immigration authorities. It was a good thing that she had with her a *Newsweek* magazine with a picture of Ninoy, and she pointed to his picture and told them that he was her father. Luckily, they believed her!

We had been shielded from the press during our stopover in Honolulu and again in San Francisco. When we arrived at the airport there, we did not go through the tube but through the stairway, and so did not get to see the media people waiting for us. Looking back, people were saying it was like what happened when Ninoy was assassinated. We were again hidden from the media.

Once we got to Dallas and checked in at the hospital, Dr. Rolly Solis instantly noticed the way Ninoy was walking and told me that he walked like a heart patient. There was so much security at the hospital. Members of the SWAT team had been posted there to guard Ninoy. The hospital staff were also so excited because important people would call, like Sen. Ted Kennedy. Ninoy was eager to eat the food even at the hospital, especially the barbecue sandwich, after a visitor from the State

Department suggested to him that he have lunch at the hospital and to try it.

On the day of the triple by-pass operation, before he was wheeled into the operating room, Ninoy called Peping aside and told him that, should he die, Peping should take care of us. The operation took about four-and-a-half hours. Ballsy and I waited in our hotel room just crying from, I suppose, a combination of tension because of the surgery and sheer exhaustion. We had not slept for, I think, two nights. Every so often, Rolly called to update us on the progress of the operation, which turned out to be successful in the end.

Ninoy was brought to the ICU after the operation, where we could visit him for short periods of five to ten minutes. While there, he had a hallucination and thought that he was back in Fort Magsaysay. He kept saying, "I won't sign. I won't sign." Rolly assured him, "No, Ninoy, I am your doctor." And Ninoy asked him, "Who is your wife?" Only when Rolly said Margie's name did Ninoy believe him.

Ninoy's triple by-pass operation was performed on May 13, a date chosen by Ninoy as it was the Feast of Our Lady of Fatima. Once again, she proved providential. It was on the very same date, five years before on May 13, 1975, that Ninoy ended his forty-day hunger strike. On the Feast of Our Lady of Fatima, Ninoy for the second time got a new lease on life.

Happiest in exile

After Ninoy's surgery, we stayed in Dallas for another twelve days so that he could rest and fully recover.

Even just after his surgery, many Filipinos from all over the US were calling him and coming to see him to apprise him of their various planned activities. Geny Lopez, Steve Psinakis, Sonny Alvarez, and Raul Manglapus were among those who came to visit him in Dallas. The Steak Commandos, they were called at that time. Raul had offered him the presidency of the Movement for a Free Philippines, but Ninoy declined the offer because Raul had already been heading it all that time. He reassured Raul, however, that he would give the movement his full support.

Just six weeks after surgery, Ninoy flew to Damascus, Syria, to meet with Nur Misuari. I was very upset with him, to say the least. For the first time in so long we were having a semblance of normalcy in our lives. I asked Rolly to please tell him that he was not well enough to make such a trip, to forbid him to go, but Rolly said that he could not lie to Ninoy. You would think that he had never, ever told a lie in his entire life! Ninoy went, but, fortunately, his health was not affected.

While we were in California for a month for his recuperation, Filipinos would also come and visit every day, sometimes staying overnight. I asked him again if he could just let things be for a while, now that we had attained some degree of normalcy in our lives, which we could enjoy. But Ninoy looked forward to these visits and to talking to all these people. And the people, I suppose, were also very eager to hear the latest from him.

All this time, we did not know how long we would be allowed to stay, or even if we would be allowed to stay on. As it turned out, Ninoy had contacted some friends who were able to work out a fellowship for him in Harvard.

During the first year, Ninoy was really happy there. Ninoy never dreamed that he would ever be able to go to Harvard, and he told friends that it was, for him, paradise. Of course, because of his incarceration, because of his seven years and seven months in detention, Harvard was only too happy to receive him and to have someone on campus with his kind of background.

While in Boston, Ninoy made the rounds of the colleges and universities where he was invited to speak and met with members of the academe as well. He talked about the dictatorship and explained to them the situation as it truly was in the Philippines. He wondered why it seemed that the US had two sets of policies regarding human rights. Human rights violations in the US would surely be swiftly condemned, but they would look the other way when these happened in a foreign country that was friendly to the US, as in the Philippines.

In the colleges and universities, the students usually reacted with shock at how their government operated. They asked Ninoy what they could do, and Ninoy suggested that they write their congressman and ask why Marcos, who was a human rights violator, was still being supported by the US government.

Even then, Ninoy would say that he felt the Americans preferred Marcos to him. Marcos was somebody who had a price tag and, because they knew what this was, they could buy him with their support. In his case, Ninoy said, he was still a question mark, a bit of an enigma to the Americans. They did not know what he really wanted. Perhaps they also felt that Ninoy no longer had a chance, or their thinking was that Marcos would hold sway forever.

Ninoy was happy in Boston, and we saw a lot more of him than we ever did before, unless he was on a speaking engagement. For the first time in a very long time, it was a normal kind of family life. He helped around the house and did a lot of driving, until he ruptured his Achilles tendon.

I refer to the three years that we were there as the happiest of my married life, because they came after the very difficult period of Ninoy's incarceration. I really liked Boston because we could live in anonymity. The Filipinos living there were professionals and members of the academe, to whom we became very close. It was also delightful that finally we could say anything that we wanted. Finally, we were having a very peaceful life.

Slowly, however, the excitement and the novelty of our life in Boston began to wear off, as far as Ninoy was concerned. The Philippines was never far from his thoughts and he wanted to be where the action was. Ninoy was never out of touch with people back home and was always current with the events happening there as he would always receive calls and visitors from Manila. One of them was Senator Tañada, who told Ninoy that if presidential elections were going to be held in 1981, then Ninoy should return home and run as the candidate. Marcos, however, changed the minimum age requirement from forty to fifty years old. Ninoy at that time was only forty-eight. This development made me the happiest person in the world, although I could not express this publicly.

Doy Laurel also came to visit. He and Ninoy decided that Doy would be the candidate instead. Doy and Senator Tañada suggested to Ninoy that he come home and help Doy with the campaign. But when they got to Tokyo, Doy called Ninoy and said that he had changed his mind. Something had come up, I do not recall what, which made it impossible for Doy to run. This of course meant that Ninoy would not have to return home, and again I was very happy about this development. As it turned out, it was Alejo Santos (former defense secretary under Pres. Carlos P. Garcia) who ran against Marcos, and of course he lost.

Then sometime in 1983 there was talk that Marcos was in poor health and he could go at any time. I think this hastened Ninoy's decision to go back. It was the general assumption then that the military would take over, or maybe Imelda first, then the military. He thought that would set us further back in our quest for democracy. Later on, when I became president, we found a file in Malacañang in which Marcos listed the names of his possible successors. It noted that his foreign affairs minister, Carlos Romulo, was too old. It also listed his former vice-president, Nanding Lopez. There were many names but, in the end, he said Imelda should be it. I forget what year Marcos wrote this, but he was in fact thinking of Imelda as the only successor to him.

Ninoy was determined to return but not to lead any fight against Marcos, anything that engaged in violence. He just wanted to have a chance to talk to Marcos and hopefully convince him that now was the time to return to democracy.

I even asked him, "Ninoy, what makes you think that Marcos would even bother to talk to you?"

But Ninoy was decided, telling me that he would still have to try. He also added, "If I don't go now, I will question myself later on. I could have done something, but why didn't I do anything? I would blame myself forever."

Later on, people would ask me, "Why didn't you stop him?" I've never stopped Ninoy when I am convinced that he wants to do the right thing or the best thing possible. For instance, I was never for him going into politics, but he believed that was what he was meant to do.

Time to go home

It was in 1983, about February, that Ninoy began saying that he really had to go home, that the people needed him there. He felt that by staying on in Boston he was becoming irrelevant. Ninoy would even ask people who came to visit what people back home were thinking. And our relatives who came over, like Baby and Terry, Esto and Maur, told him that the people realized he deserved the rest in the US, but that they wanted a leader who was highly visible. Ninoy was also thinking how one could lead effectively if one were ten thousand miles away. The perception in the Philippines that anyone who is in the US is there to enjoy life away from the suffering also did not help him any. Ninoy became more and more convinced that it was time for him to return. His mother was very much against it. But, of course, Ninoy had fully thought it over and felt that nothing would happen if he did not return and rally the people.

A month before he was to return home, even up to his last week in Boston, we would talk about possible scenarios. The first possibility, he said, was that he might be brought back to Fort Bonifacio and incarcerated again for God-knows-how-long. Second, because he had undergone heart surgery, he might be brought to the Heart Center and placed under house arrest. The authorities could also bring him back to our house in Times Street and place him under house arrest there. He said the worst thing that could happen to him was if Imelda welcomed him at the airport. In that case, his credibility would be completely shattered. The people would never believe that he had struck no deal with Marcos.

Then I asked him about the talks that, upon his return, he would be assassinated. Ninoy did not think that this would happen. Should Marcos, however, make the mistake of having him assassinated, then Ninoy said it would be the best thing that could ever happen to him. He always said that he did not want to die in the hospital, that he never wanted to grow old and be dependent on other people. He always said that what he wanted was to die for his country.

Ninoy was as determined to return home as I was reluctant to let him. Still, with a sense of inevitability, we set about the task of making preparations for his return.

The original plan was for Ninoy to return home with Noynoy and Kris on August 7, 1983. Kris had to be back in Manila in time for classes at the International School, while Noynoy was to take care of Kris in case Ninoy was arrested again. The rest of us were to follow two weeks later, as we still had the packing to do and also had to see to the selling of our house.

Ninoy had applied for a new passport, because all our passports had expired and we had not been able to renew them, but his application was denied. On the instructions of Enrile, the Philippine Consulate in New York refused to provide him with the necessary travel documents. Enrile had also instructed all the airline representatives in Manila not to allow Ninoy onto any of their flights without the proper documents. It so happened that Imelda was in New York and she granted Ninoy an appointment. Ninoy went to see her and expressed to her his desire to go home. She asked for his passport and, of course, that was the last he saw of it!

Ninoy, however, had two other passports. He had always had this extra passport, a fake one, which was acquired for him by Rashid Lucman, a congressman from Mindanao, when Ninoy saw him in Damascus. This bore the name Marcial Bonifacio, signifying for Ninoy the place, Fort Bonifacio, where he had been imprisoned on the imposition of martial law. One of his friends working in the Philippine Consulate in New Orleans had also provided him with a passport. Although this one bore his real name, it was Ballsy, and not the officials in the consulate, who filled in the data.

Then Ninoy had requested the people in Manila, through his sisters, to prepare something for his arrival. Prior to his arrival, the opposition were already meeting and planning a fitting welcome for Ninoy, so that it can gain mileage for the opposition. Doy was, I guess, spearheading the move. They thought the song "Tie a Yellow Ribbon" was an apt theme for Ninoy's homecoming. It was a song that we first heard about from the Dioknos when Pepe was still in prison. It had a line that went "Tie a yellow ribbon 'round the old oak tree. It's been three long years. Do you still want me?" The organizers wanted Ninoy to know that he was certainly still welcome in his country, and suggested that people tie yellow ribbons and wear yellow shirts. And so, back home, trees, lampposts, fences, buildings, and just about any place possible, were hung with bright yellow ribbons in anticipation of Ninoy's arrival. I did not realize, however, that it was difficult, and that it took longer, to get the color yellow in material. There was also talk that Imelda was warning the textile manufacturers. Whatever it was, it was getting more and more difficult to get the yellow material for the T-shirts.

Ninoy had also prepared his arrival statement. He showed me the first draft, where it said that he had promised Marcos that he would return and so, keeping his promise, he had. I reminded him of what he used to say, that a pact with the devil is no pact at all, and so he removed the statement. (Just goes to show that, after seven years and seven months in jail, he had learned to listen to me!) Ninoy also wrote about Gandhi's notion of non-violence. He then sent a copy of his statement to the director of the Center of International Affairs in Harvard for his comments, and he also mailed one to one of his close friends, Guy Pauker, who was with Rand Corporation. Guy was one of those friends of Ninoy's whom he listened to a lot. Guy had also been to the Philippines. He had told Ninoy that, if he were to rely on the opposition leaders in Manila, nothing would happen because they could not get their act together. Ninoy also showed what he had written to Ken Kashiwahara, the husband of Lupita.

Ninoy was not to be dissuaded, even in the face of persistent warnings about his possible assassination. Even his own mother's pleas would not deter him. She had earlier written to Ninoy to tell him that someone close to General Ver had told her that he would be killed at the airport. Enrile also sent him a telegram advising him not to come home because there were certain elements out to get him. These were supposedly the communists, who were blaming Ninoy for the deaths of those NPA witnesses during the military commission trial.

Because of the delay in getting the travel documents, plans had to be changed. In the end, Ninoy's trip was postponed to August 21. He was to return home alone, travelling a circuitous route from Boston to Los Angeles, then to Singapore, Malaysia, Hong Kong, Taipei, and finally on to Manila.

Lupita's husband, Ken, who was with ABC, was scheduled to fly with him from Taiwan. Through Kiyoshi Wakamiya, a freelance Japanese journalist, Japanese media people were contacted to accompany Ninoy on the flight home. *Time* magazine correspondent Sandra Burton was also in Taiwan to meet him. By traveling with these journalists, Ninoy thought that those allegedly plotting to kill him might abort their plan when they saw media covering his arrival.

The night before he left, I could not sleep. It was August 12 and August is a summer month, but in Boston sometimes it gets cool.

I told Ninoy, "Ninoy, I cannot sleep; I'm having chills. I'm really worried!"

He then reminded me, "Cory, we've talked about this for a long time. Anyway, this is something that I have to do." For him, the matter was settled and, of course, I realized that; but I just wanted him to know how I felt.

The following morning, we all went to church and I was really feeling sad.

Ninoy called us from Taiwan, so we more or less knew what time he was expected in Manila. Ninoy sounded fine on the phone. He also told me that he had written each one of us letters and that he had asked Noy Brizuela, who had accompanied him from Los Angeles to Taipei, to mail them to us.

In the airport, before he left, I had also reminded him, "Ninoy, *basta pag ıating na pag ıating mo ıoon, sana makatawag ka.* Or else, tell somebody in your family or my family to call me so I will know that you're back home and safe. Whatever happens, if you can call me, please call me. But if you can't, get somebody to call me so I'll know that you're there."

The best thing that could ever happen to him

In Boston, meanwhile, my children and I tried to bravely get through the long hours of waiting for word that he had finally reached home, praying, reading the Bible. I had calculated that Ninoy would arrive in Manila at about one o'clock in the afternoon, which would be about one o'clock in the morning in Boston.

I had gone to bed, but not to sleep, when at about one-thirty the phone rang. It was a Japanese correspondent from the Kyodo News Agency on the line. Ballsy, who was also still up, got the call. I heard her tell the person on the line that she did not know anything, but from the sound of her voice I knew that something was wrong.

Then, shortly after that, I got a call from the UPI. I told them that we had not heard anything, and the person on the line said, "Well, we heard there was shooting; and a reporter said that Mr. Aquino was shot!"

As my anxiety was starting to build up, I decided to seek out Arnold Zeitlin, who was the AP head in Boston then. I called him up to find out what was happening and asked if he had heard anything. Because he was a good friend of ours, I would think he would be the first to call me.

Arnold claimed that he did not know anything, but promised to let me know once he did. I found out later that he already knew, but did not want to be the one to confirm the news to me.

Then, Noynoy, who was watching CNN on television, said, "Mom, uh, *hindi pa naman* sure 'to, but it's just that there was a report *na* Dad was shot."

Cong. Shintaro Ishihara of Japan, a friend of Ninoy's, then also called. He told me that Wakamiya had called and confirmed that Ninoy had been shot. It was a fatal wound, because Ninoy had been shot in the head.

At that point, I just cried and then told my children that there was nothing else we could do except kneel down and pray. We started praying the rosary when, at about 3:30 a.m., the doorbell rang. My first thought was that they had come to get us, too. They had finished with Ninoy, and now it was our turn to die. I told Noynoy not to open the door unless he knew who it was. It turned out to be the consul general of Japan and his wife, who had been instructed by Ishihara to inform us of Ninoy's death. (They did not know that Ishihara, perhaps owing to his excitable nature, could not bear to wait and had already told us himself.) The consul general had also advised the police in Newton, where we were living, to provide us with additional security.

I also told my children to call our friends in Boston, and the doctors came bringing me all sorts of tranquilizers! People from New York, including Ernie Maceda and Sonny Alvarez, also came.

The calls came one after the other. But there was no call from Manila. I guess they did not want to call until they had actually seen the body. It took time before my mother-in-law, Lupita, and the others were able to get inside Fort Bonifacio, where Ninoy's body was brought.

While waiting, Ballsy suggested that we hear mass. "*Magsi-six o'clock na. Magsimba na tayo.*"

We lived across Boston College, so we went to the chapel there. I remember that in my prayer I was saying, "Dear Lord, I hope you can send me a Filipino priest. The American priests have been very sympathetic, but I think I'll feel better if I can talk with a Filipino priest."

At nine o'clock, our doorbell rang. Noynoy informed me that there was a priest outside, who said that his name was Fr. Catalino Arevalo and that he was from the Ateneo but was now in Boston College. I don't remember exactly if Father Arevalo was in Boston for convocation, but he said that he had heard about Ninoy and that people had told him that we lived nearby, so he thought to come to our home. Father Arevalo was also offering to say mass, which I suggested to schedule later on when some of our other friends came. Later on, I told him about my prayer, that I had prayed for a Filipino priest because I felt I could communicate better with him and that a Filipino priest can better understand what we were feeling at that moment.

Before we knew it, media people began coming by. Luckily, Noynoy was willing to face them, so I acceded and told him to go ahead.

Calls continued to come in. And, since we only had one telephone, we had to ask our neighbors if we could use their telephone because we were getting calls from everywhere.

When I was finally able to talk to my sisters, Josephine and Terry, I told them to arrange for Ninoy's body to be brought to our house in Times Street, as I felt that it would be safer for us there. I was also thinking that people would be afraid and would not want to be seen with us. I asked Maur to choose a simple coffin for Ninoy. I knew that he would not have wanted anything expensive or fancy. I also did not think a full-page obituary was necessary. A small one would do, as everybody already knew about Ninoy's death.

The next morning, Monday, a limousine came by to bring me to the TV stations of the three major networks for a round of interviews. Ken Kashiwahara's friends called to request that I appear in *Nightline* as well. Kris accompanied me to the TV station and, while we were waiting, the director came over to me and asked, "Mrs. Aquino, is it all right? I asked your daughter if she'd like to be on the show."

Kris said, "Yeah, Mom, I want!"

During the taping, I was thinking to myself, "My God, this twelve-year-old girl is so composed and ready to answer anything and everything, and here I am just praying, 'Dear Lord, help me to give the best answer possible.'"

I did not like being interviewed, did not want to be exposed to all of the media; but, at the same time, I felt that maybe this was one last thing I could do for Ninoy.

As the days passed, I would catch myself wanting to believe that it was just all a nightmare, and that I would wake up and that none of this would be true. But the reality was, it was on television.

I felt so sorry for Ninoy when I watched the footages on CNN. If Ninoy had been still alive at that time, he would have anyway ended up dead because of the rough way they handled his body. They just threw him in the van.

Ninoy had reassured me many times before he left that it would be foolish for Marcos to have him killed. But if he did, then he would do Ninoy a great service. I reminded my children of this, that he always wanted to die for the country and so his assassination was really the best thing that could ever happen to him. It sort of lessened the sorrow.

An unexpected homecoming

I was hoping that we would be able to get back on the earliest flight. Then either Terry or Passy told me that Malacañang had just announced that any airline that would take us would first have to make sure that we had valid travel documents. Our passports were not valid, however, and so Ernie Maceda had to call the consulate in New York, bring the passports there to be stamped with a one-way return trip to the Philippines, and bring them back to us in Boston. I also called the State Department, and they reassured me that we would have no problems leaving the US and that they would assist us in any way they could.

We had ourselves booked on the Tuesday morning flight. Peping had gotten us first-class tickets on Northwest Airlines. I however felt that this was inappropriate. Ninoy had just been assassinated. Why should we come back in such conspicuous style? I went to the Northwest Airlines office and told them to downgrade us to economy. They were quite incredulous at this request. Even when we boarded the plane, the staff were very insistent, saying that they could easily accommodate us in first class. But I assured them that we would be perfectly fine where we were.

The day before we were to leave, Dr. Rolly Solis told me that he would accompany the children and me to Manila. I was very grateful to him for this and told him how much of a comfort this would be. Rolly told me that he was simply keeping his promise to Ninoy, that should anything happen to Ninoy he would be there for us. Ernie Maceda told me that he had given his word to Ninoy as well. I was very much touched by these gestures, but was worried that Ernie would not be able to leave Manila anymore, unlike Rolly, who was an American citizen. But Ernie insisted and at that time, I have to admit, I was really touched by what he did.

I hardly slept throughout the flight. Our first stop was Chicago, and I had to give a press conference there. The next stop was Tokyo. There I saw the biggest assemblage of reporters and photographers I had ever yet seen. The clicking of the cameras was constant. We had never experienced anything quite like this before.

In Tokyo, I was to meet Len Oreta, Ninoy's brother-in-law, and Noy Brizuela, who would give us the letters that Ninoy entrusted to him in Taipei. As we read them, we could not stop crying. Congressman Ishihara, who was there with his wife to meet us, suggested that we photocopy the letters in case they were confiscated in Manila. Even in the midst of grieving, we had to think of, and be ready for, any possibility.

In fact, on the flight home, Ernie would pose all sorts of questions and possible scenarios to me. For instance, he asked me what I would do if Imelda or Kokoy were at the airport. Most definitely, I told him, I would not go with either one of them. As it turned out, when we got to Manila, it was Gen. Tomas Karingal who met us and asked for our passports and baggage tags.

He informed us that a room at the airport had been prepared for us where we could stay, while he took care of things. At that point, I was in a quite defiant mood, ready to fight the whole world. I told him that we could very well take care of ourselves and would rather go through the normal procedure. (So much for normal procedure, because we had twenty-four pieces of luggage! Our packing was so rushed, we just stuffed things in boxes.)

I also told him that I expected my brothers and sisters to meet us, as planned. But General Karingal said that there was no one there to meet us. It was only when we got to the baggage claim area that I saw my brothers and sisters. They had been given the run-around, told to go to a certain area then another. And they were telling us that my brothers and sisters were not even there!

From the airport, we went to see my mother. I needed to talk to her and reassure her that I was fine. Then when we got to Times Street, I saw the biggest surprise of my life. In spite of the rain, an enormous crowd had gathered at our house to pay their respects, solemnly filing past Ninoy's coffin in an endless stream. (Someone had noted the number of people passing by the coffin and counted twenty-four people on each side per minute!) It was no longer practical to keep Ninoy's body in our house. It was becoming very difficult; there were such long lines. My sister, Josephine, had earlier told me that there were suggestions that Ninoy's body be transferred instead to Santo Domingo Church.

I also did not realize that someone had put a box in our house for donations. And, in fact, when they changed Ninoy's suit, there were many coins inside the coffin. His coffin had no glass, because it was imported. Remember that I had told Maur to choose a simple coffin. This is what she chose, an imported and expensive one!

When I arrived, I requested that my children and I be left to ourselves when we looked at Ninoy's body. I did not want people to be staring at us. Maur; my brother-in-law, Paul Aquino; and Rolly were the only ones with us. People had warned me to prepare myself for a shocking sight. Ninoy's hair was matted with blood, his face was badly bruised, the eyelids blackened, and his shirt—the same one he was wearing when he was killed—was all bloody.

When I saw him, I kissed him on the lips and, for a moment, I was taken aback. It was like kissing wood. Then I remembered that, when Ninoy was in the ICU in Dallas, I would hold his hand and he would clutch my hand very tightly. So I touched his hand, it did not feel as stiff, and I started talking to him, asking him what else he wanted me to do. I could hear Rolly sobbing and, later, he said that it was a little eerie listening to me, because it was as if I were talking to someone who was alive.

Much as we wanted to be with Ninoy, I realized that we could not have all the time to linger because so many people were waiting their turn to see him. We stayed for about fifteen minutes, then my children and I retired to my room. There was not much time to rest, however, as I still had many things to attend to, people to meet.

I had to give a press conference that night. One of the things I said was that I prayed that the local media would be as courageous as the foreign media in speaking out truthfully about what had happened. Then, later on, somebody wrote that he or she had been touched by what I had said and had summoned up the courage to write about the injustice done to Ninoy and his family.

I suppose it was only after that press conference when the people became more aware of Cory Aquino. While it was true that I had given interviews when Ninoy was in prison, these were never seen by the Filipino people. Even if I had made it to the *Hong Kong Standard* and the *Bangkok Post*, the exposure then was still very minimal. Only after Ninoy's assassination, when I came out on the three major US networks and from the tremendous media coverage in Japan and then here, did people slowly get to know about me. In fact, when Ninoy's body was transferred to Santo Domingo Church, there were some instances early on when I still had to introduce myself so that I could get through the endless lines of people waiting to see Ninoy.

At Santo Domingo Church, the scene that greeted us in Times Street when we arrived was repeated here, where the lines of people snaked back as far as the eye could see. All day and all night, people shuffled past Ninoy's coffin. What amazed us was that, in spite of the great number of people, there were no disturbances. People waited patiently in line, talking quietly among themselves, orderly and disciplined.

The funeral was originally scheduled for Tuesday, August 30, 1983. But one of my Chinese *comadres*, Evelyn Lee, told me that according to their beliefs Tuesday was an inauspicious day for holding funerals. I do not really believe in such things, but my friend insisted that I do it for the sake of my children at least. Besides, what was a delay of one day? So I agreed to postpone the funeral to Wednesday, the thirty-first.

We had brought Ninoy's body to Tarlac that Saturday, August 27. On

Monday, the day we were going back to Manila to bring his body back to Santo Domingo Church, the people of Central Luzon were requesting that we stop by the towns so that they could see Ninoy. Fearing that this would cause too much of a delay, I instead agreed to their request that we pass McArthur Highway instead of the expressway so that they could at least catch a glimpse of Ninoy's hearse. The night before we left, however, the people of Concepcion, Tarlac, also requested that we pass by their town because Ninoy had been mayor there. I agreed to do so even if I knew that this detour would add more hours to our drive home.

It was in Tarlac that I saw for the first time T-shirts being sold. T-shirts with the saying Ninoy, *hindi ka nag-iisa* (you are not alone), The Filipino is worth dying for, and the like. (Incidentally, the slogan "Ninoy, *hindi ka nag-iisa*" was the brainchild of Nina Kalaw-Puyat, the sister of Eva Kalaw and a relative of Ninoy's.) I must admit that, initially, this upset me. My thinking was, why were people out to make money from a tragedy such as this? In time, however, I realized that on my own I would not have been able to have those T-shirts made and simply given away. Also, the fact that people were willing to buy them and put themselves at risk by possibly incurring the ire of the dictatorship helped me to look at it in a different way. While it was true that some people were making money, the enterprise was indeed helping to spread awareness of the cause and getting people involved in the struggle.

I was also, in the beginning, upset by the jokes. Filipino culture being what it is, there were numerous jokes, one of which was that when Ninoy died and went up to Heaven, Rolando Galman (the man alleged by the government to be Ninoy's assassin) was already there waiting for him and telling him, "*Pare, ang tagal-tagal mo naman*" (You took so long.), implying that Galman had already been dead when he was brought to the airport. We had already lost a loved one, and people were still making jokes. Later, I reasoned to myself that the Filipino people were just being true to their nature. They were not being intentionally disrespectful. It was simply their usual way of coping with adversity, using humor.

In almost every big town in Central Luzon, we had to stop. There were so many people that they just blocked the hearse. Sometimes there would be a priest who would bless Ninoy's body. In other places, they would release doves or sing "Bayan Ko." It was a most extraordinary experience for us all. It took us eleven hours to get back to Santo Domingo Church from Tarlac. And this, without eating or drinking!

I had also received a similar request that Ninoy's body be brought to the Visayas and Mindanao. Some people were saying that I owed this to the Filipino people; since they could not come and see Ninoy, he should be brought to them. I, however, just wanted to bring Ninoy to his final resting place, so that also we, his family, could take a rest after such a long ordeal. Some people were also saying that this was one way we could gather crowds. I did not think that this was the right thing to do. They even coursed this request through the people who they thought had influence over me, like Sr. Christine Tan and some politicians. But I had already made up my mind. I was not about to turn Ninoy's wake into a circus.

Coming back to Manila, I remember the most impressive scene was at the Balintawak Monument. From where we were sitting in our van, I could not see the road. It seemed that the road had simply disappeared as every available space was occupied by the huge crowds. My mother-in-law, seeing this, commented that it was unfortunate that Ninoy had died before people could express their love for him. She said that if only even just a few thousand of the millions of Filipinos who went to see him in death had told him how much they cared for him, it would have helped lessen his load while he was still alive.

Still, tired as we were, we felt consoled seeing all those people and all those signs again saying things like *Hindi ka nag-iisa*. Finally, it seemed that people were appreciating all that Ninoy had done for them. Whereas before I thought that Ninoy had been forgotten, that no one seemed to care about all the sufferings he went through, more and more I felt that apparently this was not so. I had met this one man in Tarlac who was extremely helpful to us, and I was very grateful to him for that. He told me that there was no need to thank him, that Ninoy had done so much for his fellowmen and I was merely reaping the benefits of his kindness. In Tagalog they say, "*Ina-ani mo 'yung tinanim ni* Ninoy."

The next day, Tuesday, I went on the air at Radio Veritas to ask the people to join us at the funeral on Wednesday and to appeal to them not to commit any violent acts. I said that Ninoy would have just wanted all of us to pray for him and for the country.

A glimpse of people power

The funeral mass was scheduled for nine o'clock in the morning, but I was in church as early as seven o'clock. And if I were not Cory Aquino, I probably would not have been able to enter. People had apparently not bothered to leave the church from the night before, and some of them had probably even slept there. I found it next to impossible to get inside.

Inside the church, I spotted, among the diplomatic corps, US Ambassador Michael Armacost. I think the Spanish ambassador was there as well. I was appreciative of their presence, because I knew that the Ministry of Foreign Affairs had made known that the government would not look kindly upon any ambassador who would attend the funeral mass.

During the mass, I felt very sad and prayed that I would not break down so that I would be able to deliver my piece at the end. Cardinal Sin officiated and delivered such a moving homily that the people could not keep themselves from applauding. I was thinking how Ninoy would have been so happy being accorded such an honor by the Filipino people.

It was with much difficulty that we got out of the church and into our van. People were crowding around us, wanting to touch the coffin, wanting to touch my children and me. In fact, Ballsy and Pinky, who were holding two orchid sprays they were planning to put on Ninoy's coffin, ended up with just the ribbons! And Noynoy, who was not supposed to be riding atop the ten-wheeler truck with Ninoy's coffin, found himself being lifted up by these waves of people. So with Apeng Yap and Paul Aquino. Up to this day, they do not know how they got there. When I saw Noynoy up in the truck, I wondered what he was doing there. Still, I thought it was fitting that he was with his dad to accompany him on his last journey.

It had been Peping's idea to place Ninoy's coffin on a ten-wheeler truck. He recalled that time when we transported Ninoy's body to Tarlac and had had some trouble with the hearse. People were climbing up the hearse and jumping on it. I do not know if it is some kind of belief of theirs that by being that close to Ninoy they could imbibe his spirit. I could not believe my eyes, confronted by such a strange sight. When we got to Tarlac, the hearse had to be replaced. Even the bumpers were found to be missing.

Perhaps the reason people clambered on top of the hearse was that they could not see the coffin. By using a ten-wheeler truck, the coffin would be elevated and exposed to all. Ninoy's cousin, Budji Layug, then had the coffin blanketed with yellow chrysanthemums or daisies. He had taken this upon himself, without my knowledge, and I felt very grateful to him for this thoughtful act.

Butz Aquino, my brother-in-law, and the August Twenty-One Movement (ATOM) had planned what route we were going to take to Manila Memorial Park from Santo Domingo Church. The route they had chosen was one where many people could converge and see the truck. From the church, we passed first through Quezon Avenue, then in front of the Legislative Building, where Ninoy had spent four years when he was senator. We had heard earlier on Radio Veritas that lightning had struck and killed a man in Luneta Park, one of the thousands congregated there waiting for Ninoy. When we passed the Luneta, we stopped and saw that someone had lowered the flag to half-staff.

Everything was all so spontaneous; there was no overall director. Along the way, people were singing "Ama Namin" and "Bayan Ko," with no prodding. As it was getting dark, I even heard on the radio that people were requesting that Ninoy's body be brought to Baclaran Church and kept there overnight. When we got to the South Expressway, we were met by a beautiful sight. People had lit candles all along that long stretch of highway.

Everywhere we went, we were met by a sea of people, even when it rained, uncomplaining of the long wait to catch just a glimpse of Ninoy's coffin. Some even abandoned their vehicles and just walked. Chino Roces was one of them.

The funeral cortege had to practically inch its way through, but finally made it to Manila Memorial Park at nine o'clock in the evening, eleven hours after it first set out from Santo Domingo Church. And, again, no one at that time thought there would be thousands upon thousands of people at the Manila Memorial Park.

All of us were very much comforted by the sight of so many people risking so much to be there for Ninoy. That's why I also make it a point to visit many wakes or attend funeral masses, because I know how much comfort the family of the deceased derives from such gestures.

Bishop Leonardo Legaspi and Father Olaguer gave Ninoy the last blessing. Then Noynoy asked to look at his dad one last time, so we opened the coffin and the children and I took one last look. Somebody handed us *sampaguita* garlands, and we put these on Ninoy's coffin.

I was glad that I had been able to bring Ninoy to his final resting place, and that everything had turned out well.

It had been a long, incredible day. I had had no breakfast, lunch, or dinner, but felt no great hunger. We were simply too overwhelmed by the show of support of the people, emotionally uplifted by it, and greatly appreciative of the sacrifices they made to see Ninoy to his final resting place. Many of them had even walked great distances because there were no means of public transportation that day, the government's idea being to discourage people from attending the funeral. Later on, the Marcos dictatorship suddenly fielded army trucks and offered free transportation to the people who had attended the funeral. However, a great many refused because, I suppose, they were worried that they would instead be taken elsewhere.

We were likewise concerned that there would be demonstrations and riots the night of the funeral, as there were reports of people burning tires around the University Belt that night. A year or so afterwards, I was being blamed by some people who said that if only I had led them, or allowed them to march to Malacañang that night, we would have much sooner seen the end of Marcos. I replied that perhaps that would have been so, but that while I was prepared to risk my life, I was not prepared to risk everyone else's life. What would we have accomplished then? That night, all I wanted was to lay Ninoy to rest, give him the peace that he deserved, and try to make life as near normal as I could for my children and me.

After the funeral, the traditional nine days of prayer followed. In addition to the wake, from August 21 to 31, where many masses were said every day, we had novena masses from September 1 to 9. And, every night, Santo Domingo Church was again filled to overflowing. We invited several priests to say mass and the homilies no longer centered solely on Ninoy. The masses offered an opportunity to openly talk about the dictatorship, the sufferings of the Filipino people, the loss of freedom, and provided a convenient forum for people who were angry with Marcos. Someone also suggested that we commemorate the fortieth day of Ninoy's death. For this occasion, we had mass at the Santuario de San Antonio in Forbes Park, Makati, followed by a procession and the praying of the rosary. I suppose it was another chance to gather people and enlist their sympathy and support for the cause of democracy.

CHAPTER III

Resistance & Revolution
1983 – 1986

Who killed Ninoy?

There were obviously many questions surrounding Ninoy's assassination. And it did not help any that some people were circulating all these stories, wild speculations that others freely believed. For instance, when I had just arrived from the States, Tony Lopez of *Asiaweek* told me some people were saying that Ninoy's assassination was actually a suicide. Some people were circulating stories that Ninoy had asked the communists to send Galman to shoot him. Tony told me that he had also heard talk of Ninoy telling Imelda that he felt he did not have long in this world because of his heart condition. I told Tony that Ninoy's bypasses were still in very good condition, and even the pathologists who performed the autopsy on him saw that this was so. I found all that talk very pathetic and stupid as well.

But what troubled me most after the assassination was that history would give credence to the story of the Marcoses that Ninoy was in fact killed by Galman. As it was, some people at that time were still inclined to believe the official line, that Galman actually was the killer. And this despite the discrepancies in the government's version of events. For one thing, there were 1,200 military men inside the airport, so it was nearly impossible for anyone to go in there and penetrate the security forces unrecognized. Someone had also observed that there was very little blood on Galman, when he was supposedly shot twenty or thirty times, while Ninoy, who had been shot just once, was bathed in a pool of blood. It was so important to me, therefore, to find people who were on the same plane with Ninoy and who could testify that the assassin was not Galman. I wanted to meet anyone who could tell me something differently from what the Marcoses were trying to impose on us.

Then, a month or so after the funeral, Peping told me that one of his friends had been able to make contact with this woman who had been on the same plane and had supposedly seen something. She lived in San Fernando, Pampanga, and, because people were still in fear of doing anything that would anger the Marcoses, she insisted that we meet at night.

Because everything had to be done in total secrecy, Peping and I, together with Ballsy and Noynoy, first went to Peping's friend's house, where we left our car. I was also advised not to wear black so that I would not be recognizable. (In fact, I even brought a kerchief to put over my head. But, as Ballsy observed, I only made myself more conspicuous that way!) We rode in a jeepney, and finally arrived at this woman's house very late at night. She and her husband refused to turn on the lights, and so we talked in total darkness.

She said that she did not see the actual shooting, but that it seemed to her that Ninoy had been hit on the head (*"pinukpok"*) by one of the men in khaki. We ourselves had been, in fact, also thinking that Ninoy had really first been struck before they shot him.

I told her that I understood her fear of putting this account down in writing. But I told her that perhaps she could nonetheless write her testimony down and keep it in a safe place, if she did not want to give it to me. It was just so important to me that I hold on to some evidence that the Marcos ploy that it was Galman was just not true. I told her that I was making this request for the sake of my children, and so that the Filipino people would know the truth.

Marcos then decided to form a committee to investigate the assassination, headed by Justice Enrique Fernando. I refused to participate in this investigation, as I did not think the outcome of it would be anywhere near the truth. This committee was eventually dissolved, and another commission was formed, headed by Corazon Agrava. I, however, still refused to participate. And it was just as well, because this commission concluded its investigation by absolving General Ver and all of the military of knowledge and responsibility in the assassination of Ninoy.

I issued a statement immediately after this conclusion came out. I pointed out that in anything that concerned Ninoy, it was Marcos who always made the decisions. Only *he* planned what should be done to Ninoy. I cited many instances of this from our experience in the past. For example, when Ninoy was transferred to Fort Magsaysay, Enrile had said that he had no knowledge of this. (Well, I do not know if he had been lying then.) Also, during the military tribunal proceedings, one never knew when the rules were going to be changed. It was always Marcos orchestrating everything.

I truly believe that it was Marcos, and no one else, who ordered the killing of Ninoy.

Pepe Diokno had always been convinced that it could only be Marcos, and not anyone else, not even Imelda. Some people were saying that Marcos was in poor health and could not have planned the assassination. But Pepe argued that Marcos was a lawyer, and a brilliant one at that. Such lawyers, he said, know how to plant the necessary alibis. This was something Marcos had always been good at. And, in fact, prior to the assassination, he had been spreading the word around that he was sick. He may have been sick, but not while he was planning the assassination, and not while it happened.

Then rumors had it that Imelda had said to let the Aquinos have their day, because anyway, after a month, the Filipino people would forget. This was one time, however, that they did not forget.

Perhaps this was also because, after Ninoy's assassination, the Philippine economy took a turn for the worse. Shortly after the assassination, the Philippine government issued a moratorium on our debt payments. As a result of this, we lost all our standing credits and everything had to be paid for in cash. People began to hoard basic necessities. Long lines at the supermarkets became a common sight, as those who could afford them would buy and stock up on canned goods.

The farthest thing from my mind

When I look back on what has happened thus far in my life, I begin to realize that all the trials my family and I were made to undergo were to prepare us to face the many challenges ahead. If, early on, someone had foretold what my life would be like, I would have said that I would go mad. But this is probably one of my greatest strengths, that in the most crucial periods in my life I did not break and collapse. These periods, in fact, brought me closer to God and made me a more firm believer.

Really and truly, I thought that after the funeral and the nine days of prayer I could go back to my private life, and that my children and I could try to make life as near to normal as we could. When I was still in Boston, foremost in my mind was just to get home and give Ninoy a decent funeral. If the opposition needed my help, then I would help them; but it would be a limited kind of support. I did not envision myself giving speeches, or being the candidate. That was the farthest thing from my mind.

I never harbored any personal political ambitions. In fact, in the beginning, some of my decisions were based on instinct. For instance, when I heard that Marcos wanted to express his condolences, I said that if he were really sincere he should prove it by releasing all political prisoners. My vocation was, and always had been, to the family. However, as the succeeding events in my life would reveal, I found myself extending this vocation to later include the bigger family—the Filipinos, the country. I suppose I was then merely defining the role God had planned for me. So many things are possible with prayer and faith in God to support us.

After the funeral, members of the Aquino family were invited around the country to speak about Ninoy. My mother-in-law was a much sought-after speaker, as was Butz, who, in his speeches, talked about the assassination and expressed the belief that Marcos was responsible for this dastardly deed.

I did not give my first speech until October. Up until then, I felt that I was not ready. The Concerned Women of the Philippines had invited me to address them, together with Cecilia Muñoz-Palma, and this was the first time I spoke publicly. It can be said that this marked my entry into public life.

We would speak in different places, telling the story over and over again. To me, and others close to me, it might have sounded very repetitive. But in many different fora, that was the first time they had heard about Ninoy's experience, in particular his being transferred to Fort Magsaysay in Nueva Ecija. Whenever I recounted the sufferings that Ninoy had to undergo, and that I had to undergo, this was something very new to them. It made them realize how much hardship Ninoy had to experience in order to provide the Filipino people with an alternative to Marcos and communism.

Apart from giving speeches, I also began to participate in the rallies organized to protest Ninoy's assassination and to pursue his dream of democracy. Every Friday in Makati's business district, the people marched down the streets in ever increasing numbers, amid a flurry of yellow confetti (piling ankle-deep in places) and applause and cheers. People were, I guess, becoming bolder.

The United Nationalist Democratic Organization (UNIDO) was also at this time trying to organize itself, having in mind the Batasang Pambansa elections scheduled for 1984. Its members offered me the position of vice-president for Central Luzon, an offer I declined, saying that I would simply support them in other ways. I remember that both Senator Tañada and Soc even spoke up in one UNIDO meeting and told its members that I had already undergone enough hardships and must not be further imposed upon.

Much of my time was also spent giving interviews. Many foreign correspondents were in the country and I thought it favorable that we were still able to project ourselves internationally. But it was not until a year after the funeral that I granted my first television interview. This was on Dong Puno's show *Viewpoint*. This was also the first time I was asked if I was thinking of becoming the presidential candidate, of being drafted as one. Trying to make a joke of it, I answered that in the Philippines there were no drafts, only typhoons. In truth, the thought was farthest from my mind. As I said, I was not even thinking of accepting the position of vice-president of the UNIDO, much less president of the entire country.

Suddenly, from being so unpopular before, we became such a hot item after Ninoy's assassination. In the *Mr. and Ms. Magazine*, it seemed that every week there was an Aquino featured there. I also thought it would be difficult to get a passport back to the States for the memorial service of Ninoy in Harvard in November. But there was no problem at all. I think the Marcoses were just too glad that I was leaving and probably preferred that I stay abroad.

A number of the opposition were also meeting. They approached me with a request that I sign this document specifying certain demands that, if not met, would lead us to boycott the Batasang Pambansa elections in 1984. I asked them why I should sign when I did not represent any organization, as the other signatories did. I do not know why I allowed myself to sign up. But they prevailed upon me, and so I agreed. And this, as it turned out, was one of the biggest mistakes of my life, as I did not believe in boycotting the elections.

Marcos, naturally, did not give in to the opposition's demands, prompting the opposition members to call for a nationwide boycott of the elections. Not fully convinced that this is what we should do, I went through a period of soul-searching and many sleepless nights. I kept hoping Ninoy would appear to me in a dream and tell me what to do! I guess he just wanted me to think for myself.

In the end, it all came down to me wanting to be true to myself. I could not, I felt, honestly stand on a stage and appeal to the people to boycott, when I myself did not believe in it. That would have been, for me, an impossible stance. I told them that I was sorry, but that I would participate.

The first time I was hinting at this was when I spoke before the Manila Rotary Club. I had asked Mon del Rosario to help me with my speech, and he could sense right away without my saying so that I was for participating in the elections. Mon was actually for boycotting it but, because I had asked him to help me in my speech, he had to write it the way I wanted it.

Later on, I had to explain myself on Radio Veritas, explain my reasons for participating, and ask for forgiveness from the Filipino people for having changed my original position. I had asked the advice of Fr. Joaquin Bernas on this, and I also thought that only a fool would continue to be tied down to an earlier commitment, if you could even call it that, when there was a better option available. Also, it was not as if I would be the only one to profit from participating, as I was not even a candidate.

I suppose this—my not being a candidate—was proof that I had no ulterior motive. Still, I was not spared receiving a number of truly nasty letters! Someone wrote that Ninoy was probably turning in his grave because of what I had done. Others were saying that it was because I was just a housewife, so what could one expect from me. They said I was so naive, that I did not realize that by participating in it I was only lending credence to elections that would again no doubt be marred by cheating. In fairness to them, Pepe, Jovy, and Senator Tañada never said anything nasty against me. It was actually the lesser lights, whom I will not be bothered to name, and may God forgive them!

With regard to my in-laws, Butz and Maur were against participation, while Paul was for it. My mother-in-law expressed regret that Butz and I did not agree on this issue. I told her I was sorry as well, but that I felt this was what had to be done. She was very understanding and, later on, even helped me in the campaign for participation.

My decision was not based on a whim. I had my reasons for participating. First, Ninoy had always believed that Filipinos love elections. I had always heard him say that. In fact, as we soon found out, people from all over the country were indeed wanting to participate and give these elections a chance. Second, the elections could again provide the opposition with a forum, where they would be free to speak out and inform the people not only about what happened to Ninoy, but also about what was actually happening in our country.

The leaders of the opposition would always remind me that by participating I would be in the company of Marcos people. And of course this was true, because some of the candidates were in fact identified with Marcos. Still, I pointed out, after the assassination of Ninoy, these people had immediately had a change of heart, that they appeared, at least to me, sincere in wanting to help the opposition.

Practically speaking, I also felt that we could not merely rely on people who have never had anything to do with Marcos, because for certain our numbers would be few. We would be lucky to have even ten thousand people. The fact of the matter was Marcos had been in power for years, and so our national leaders have all been at one time or another connected with him. Pepe was a Nacionalista, together with Marcos. Senator Tañada, the same thing. Jovy was with Marcos when Marcos was a Liberal. All of them had to do with Marcos; all, except Ninoy.

For me the question then was: Could we manage at all if we merely confined ourselves to people who never had any dealings with Marcos during martial law?

This, I think, can be considered my first major decision, politics-wise. Against the advice of some of my fellow oppositionists, I went ahead and campaigned for participation.

The campaign took me all over the country. Outside of Metro Manila, it was in Cebu where I was much impressed with the opposition, especially with Inday Nita Daluz, who was a member of parliament previously and who became a congresswoman after the snap elections. It was she who introduced me in Cebu, because I guess she was the outstanding opposition leader, and a woman at that. The opposition there was well organized, very vocal, and active.

During the campaign, I had to raise the candidates' hands rather frequently. I found this very awkward and most unattractive for a woman to do. I wondered if we could just stand together and pose, but, in any case, I had to do it.

Someone had also warned me about one of the "perils" of campaigning—the insects that get attracted to the light of the bulbs on the stage. As you speak, sometimes you get to swallow an insect or two! I found this to be very true and would try to stay as far away as possible from the lights, but there were instances when this was simply impossible.

There was also a time when the lights went out, and all we could do was just stand there on stage and wait until they could bring the lights back on again.

Throughout the campaign, I was required to speak many times in one day. The content of my speech was basically the same and, in fact, from hearing it countless times, my driver had already memorized it and knew when it would be over. He was also aware that, when it rained, my speech would be shortened and he was familiar with this version as well.

My speech dwelt on the story of Ninoy's incarceration and assassination. In it, I also encouraged the people to do more for the country so that we could once again enjoy our rights and freedoms, and told them that even if I was "just a woman" I was willing to offer my life for the country, like Ninoy did.

Campaigning was an exhausting and yet at the same time enriching experience. It gave me the chance to relate with the people and know their thoughts, their hopes, their fears. In the end, it was rewarding as well. We were lucky that the opposition won sixty out of two hundred seats in the Batasan. Considering that there was cheating, this result was beyond anyone's expectations. It also made people realize that, by organizing and getting their act together, we could stand a chance at victory.

At that time, I did not imagine that participating in the 1984 elections would be a preparation for the snap elections, because no one was talking about snap elections yet. But, in hindsight, I think that it, in a way, provided the opposition with the groundwork for organizing throughout the country and gave the National Movement for Free Elections (NAMFREL) a first and valuable experience in the monitoring of votes.

Only on two conditions

Not too long after the Batasang Pambansa elections, people began to wonder about what to do to prepare for the elections in 1987 or the snap elections that might be called before that date.

It was then, in 1984, that the idea of forming a Convenor Group arose, whose aim was to be able to fast track a way of selecting the opposition standard bearer. This was in a way an inspired idea because the state of the opposition was still less than ideal. While it was true that we were united against Marcos, the opposition was still fragmented. Each person had his own agenda, and it seemed people were finding it hard to trust one another.

I was asked to be one of the convenors, but I immediately refused. The people who asked me were those who were instrumental in making me sign that fateful statement regarding the boycotting of the elections and, naturally, I was wary. They then approached Baby Lopa, my brother-in-law, for help in convincing me. What Baby told me was that the opposition would not convene without me, that nothing would be accomplished if I did not agree.

When I finally did, I joined Senator Tañada and Jimmy Ongpin as the convenors. We called our first meeting in December of 1984 and invited what we called the PSBs, the potential standard bearers. Actually, we had already prepared our list, but eventually had to expand this as Senator Tañada had been approached by some who felt that they should be included as well. It was amazing how many people thought of themselves as presidentiables!

The group had quite a shaky start, with Doy, who was considered a potential standard bearer, and Eva Kalaw withdrawing from the group and deciding to carry on with the UNIDO. Their reason for doing so was because there were some in the group who were against allowing the US bases to extend their stay in the country, and Doy and Eva did not agree with that.

The time also came when I found myself at odds with the members of the group. It had to do with UNIDO inviting me to attend its National Conference and me accepting the invitation. I had announced this intention to the members of the Convenor Group during one of our weekly meetings. During the meeting, Senator Tañada, Jovy, and the other men (most of them anyway) flatly told me that I could not go. They felt that, by my going there, it would make the Convenor Group appear like it was part of the UNIDO. I said that I was being invited for myself, in my personal capacity, and that it was not as if I were going to sign some document or other that would tie down the Convenor Group to the UNIDO.

As they continued to stress to me that I could not go, I felt very angry. Then the worst thing happened. Tears started welling up in my eyes! And I could not keep them from falling. Later on, Alran Bengzon told me that Jimmy, who was sitting next to me, started motioning to the others that my tears were falling. Baby, I guess, also saw it. So, suddenly, all conversation, all argument, stopped.

They realized how angry I was, angry enough to be moved to tears. And I was very upset with myself as well. How could I cry in front of all of these men!

Then Baby came up to me and said that Senator Tañada wanted to see me. The first thing I told Senator Tañada was that I would like to resign from the Convenor Group. I cited an agreement that we had, that after a certain period of time we would reassess whether or not the Convenor Group should continue to be. That deadline was approaching, and I wanted out. He asked me if I was still angry, and I told him that I was.

When the Convenor Group met in my house again, Senator Tañada informed the members that I had prepared a statement that I wanted to share with them. According to Ballsy, who was in my room about twenty meters away, my voice sounded so clear and strong.

I started off by saying that I wanted to quit. I could not understand why they would not allow me to attend the UNIDO conference. All I wanted was to keep communication lines open with UNIDO and show them that we were together in the fight for the restoration of democracy. I was also certainly not going to do anything that would commit the Convenor Group to the UNIDO. Maybe they were indeed smarter than me, I continued, having gone to Harvard and all those prestigious schools, and maybe they did have the right answers ninety-five percent of the time. But five percent of the time I, too, had the right answers. Furthermore, I made it clear to them that I would not allow anyone to tell me not to do something that I truly believed in. If, as they always said, I was so important to the group, why would they not give weight to what I believed I should do?

For the first time, all these men were quiet—in fact, Mon del Rosario commented that you could hear a pin drop—because, before, I would just sit there, be very polite, and accept whatever it was they were dishing out.

After a while, Jimmy spoke up and apologized for the group, saying they realized they had not given me the role that I deserved. I think Senator Tañada and he had discussed this beforehand, but Jimmy said that they had come up with a plan, whereby Celing Muñoz-Palma, representing UNIDO, and I, representing the Convenor Group, would try to work out a formula for choosing a presidential candidate in case of snap elections. This plan, however, never really came to anything.

First of all, UNIDO wanted a larger share of the votes in the convention for nominating the presidential candidate. The reason for this was that they felt they were the best organized and had, in fact, members of parliament who belonged to UNIDO. The Partido Demokratiko Pilipino-Lakas ng Bayan (PDP-LABAN) also wanted a bigger share, justifying this by saying that they were in existence longer. The non-government organizations (NGOs) also wanted the same thing. And, granted that there were many NGOs, how should the votes be allocated? In other words, what percentage is the NGO entitled to? How does the NGO prove its membership?

These were some of the concerns that Celing and I had to try to resolve. We worked out possible formulas but, in the end, she made no headway with her group, and neither did I with mine.

All this time, as I found out much later, Senator Tañada had in mind me as the presidential candidate. It was during an interview with French television that I found this out, when the interviewer asked me what I thought of Senator Tañada's proposal that I be the presidential candidate because, according to him, I alone could unite the opposition.

Then people like Neptali Gonzales, Celing, and others also stated that they were for me. Even Monching, if I recall correctly, told me that he would give way only to me and to no other candidate. Some people also worried that, having more than one presidential candidate, the opposition would stand no chance of winning. They argued that it was difficult enough as it was to challenge Marcos one-on-one. Having more than one candidate would cause further rifts and divisions among the opposition and, in effect, would mean handing the presidency over to Marcos on a silver platter.

Chino Roces and others had earlier advised me that I should refrain from saying outright that I would not run. They said that many of the people who had joined the opposition did so because they were encouraged by the thought that I would be the candidate. If I dashed their hopes, they might decline to help the opposition, and there would be nothing to galvanize these different groups. Again, it seemed that my role was to awaken the people and make sure that they continued to fight.

In October of 1985, while I was addressing the sorority of Betty Go-Belmonte, a question arose during the open forum about whether or not there would be any situation at all where I would consider running for the presidency.

When that question came up, Chino's advice came to mind and so I did not immediately say no. What I answered was that maybe I would, on two conditions—if snap elections were called and if a million signatures of support were collected and presented to me. I also emphasized that these conditions must occur simultaneously, that it could not be just one or the other. It was my thought that these conditions would be difficult to meet. Therefore I felt quite assured that, by imposing these conditions, I would be spared from having to run for the presidency.

Did I have to accept this cross?

Sometime in November 1985, however, I got a call at one-thirty in the morning from Ken Kashiwahara in San Francisco. He informed me that President Marcos had just announced on American television that he was going to call for snap elections! What drove him to do so I can only make a conjecture. The Philippine economy at that time was doing very poorly, and Marcos was of course totally dependent on the Americans to help him in our economy. His ace was that we had Clark Air Base and Subic Naval Base. The Americans, in turn, really needed Clark and Subic because of the Cold War. I suppose he may have been prevailed upon by the Americans to legitimize his presidency by seeking a new mandate. And, I suppose, Marcos was just so confident that he had everything under his control and that he could still win. Even if he did not win because of the popular vote, he could still manipulate the election returns to his favor.

When I heard Ken's news, I must have been the saddest person in the world!

Very early on that day, the leaders of the opposition gathered in Celing's house to plan their next move. After this meeting, I remember I called my relatives and friends and told them to inhibit themselves from joining the signature-gathering campaign. I said that, if they wanted to remain my friends, they should not sign! I also encouraged them to advise other people not to sign.

I remember during one meeting, Joe Concepcion brought in somebody from UP who was very knowledgeable about surveys, and who knew what the issues were regarding the elections and what would be most attractive to the class *C* and *D* crowds. He gave us a presentation, from which I gathered that the masses really just identified with very concrete projects, like jobs and having a roof over their heads. If such were the case, I thought the opposition did not have much of a chance because we were offering something abstract—democracy, truth, justice. We were not offering them a roof over their heads and such. Only Marcos had the resources to address these needs. It would help tremendously if we were able to give these people money. But where would the money come from? Again, only Marcos had the money.

We heard mass for my mother, who passed away July 10, at her tomb on the tenth of every month. At this particular mass in November, we had a priest from Tarlac. Over lunch, I asked him if the people understood abstracts like democracy and freedom, because I was told that they did not. He assured me that they did, but that I must present them with personalities who symbolized these things. For instance, Marcos would symbolize the injustice and all the ills of our country. The opposite of this would be Ninoy, who was a victim of this injustice. All these abstracts had to be represented by personalities to make them easier to grasp by the people.

Mulling these things over, I thought to myself that, although I may not be the worst victim of human rights violations, the fact of the matter was that I was the best known. I called Fr. Catalino Arevalo and told him that I wanted to go on a one-day retreat with the Pink Sisters.

I spent the whole day, from 9:00 a.m. to 6:00 p.m., praying before the Blessed Sacrament. I prayed for Marcos, for the leaders of the opposition, for my children, for myself. Everything seemed to be pointing to the fact that I had to agree to this draft to be presidential candidate. And yet I knew that accepting it would present many difficulties, not only for me, but also for my family. It was quite a soul-wrenching experience. Even if events were pointing to that direction, towards me having to run for president, did I have to accept this cross? I thought that being a politician's wife was difficult enough.

But I was also thinking of what Ninoy would have done and remembered what he said in an interview with Teddy Benigno while in exile. Ninoy said that he was determined to return to the Philippines, even with the real threat of death hanging over him, because he would not be able to live with himself knowing he could have done something for the country, but did not do anything about it, did not even try.

I also thought back on a dinner in Winnie Monsod's house. Johnny Collas, her brother (also a lawyer from San Francisco who was in law school with Ninoy and a good friend of his), had asked then why I didn't consider being the presidential candidate. Of course I told him I wasn't interested. Later, he wrote to me from the States. He did not want to add to my worries, he wrote, but did I not think that I might experience guilt if I did not run against Marcos? If Marcos won again, he continued, would I not think that perhaps I could have done something then and made a difference? And he said that he did not want to add anymore to my problems!

Recalling Ninoy's words and Johnny's letter, it really hit me. How could I just ignore things and say that I had suffered enough? Even if I did not think I could win against Marcos, I realized the trying would be what mattered most.

The businessmen, like Jimmy, and the politicians, like Monching and Jovy, made it also clear to me that if I did not run, I should not count on them to help Doy. Even the NGOs were of the same mind. I do not know if they orchestrated this, but it was adding so much more pressure on me. I was thinking that if these businessmen, who were in a position to help, would turn their backs and ignore the elections, nothing at all would be accomplished.

I emerged from that one-day retreat crying, and I told the nuns that it seemed that I really had to run. I suppose this was the first and only time that a presidential candidate reacted that way!

When I told the politicians and businessmen about my decision, they were, I think, relieved. I, however, was feeling so sad and just kept praying. And when I told my mother-in-law, her reaction was to also cry. She was thinking about how we have already been through so many difficult times, and again this time will be very difficult for the children and me. In the end, however, she assured me that she would be glad to be of help if there was anything she could do.

I told my children. Ballsy felt that it was unfair to be made to suffer more. I told her that I used to think the same, but had come to realize that one never really stops suffering, that only when one dies can one think of having had his quota of suffering filled. I reminded them about the blessings that we had all received in our lives. They may not win any beauty contests, I said, but they were not bad looking. When it came to brains, although none of them were summa cum laude, they were also above average in intelligence. I told them that their dad and I had a good marriage and that, maybe compared to ninety percent of the Filipino people, we have had so much more. I explained to them that nothing is for free in this world, and I believe that we have to share the blessings we have received. Of course, among all my children, it was only Kris who encouraged me to go for it. She was fourteen at that time.

Having made my decision, I immediately had to immerse myself in structuring and organizing the campaign, building a team, raising funds because, in the beginning, we were very hard up.

Peping met with the politicians and all those who helped in 1984. Jimmy, Baby, Tony Gonzales, and some others were in charge of raising funds. Teddy Boy Locsin was in charge of the media bureau. Rene Saguisag became my spokesman. Alran Bengzon was in charge of another group.

These people had assured me early on that I need not worry about anything because they would handle everything for me. They said all I had to do was go around the country and deliver speeches. Famous last words! Because when the time came to solicit major contributions, I had to approach the people concerned myself. Others would make the preliminary contact, but the people who were making the contribution wanted to give it directly to me. There were times then when I had to leave the campaign trail to meet with these would-be contributors. I found these moments very embarrassing. It helped though that someone would already tell these contributors in advance how much was needed. I really could not see myself mentioning an amount to these people and, in fact, I would never even open the envelope to see the amount of contribution made.

In the beginning, the businessmen were holding back because they did not agree to the opposition having two candidates. This was the time when Doy and I were both projecting ourselves as presidential candidates. To settle the matter, Soc was assigned to mediate between Doy and me. Doy could not understand my change of mind, why I at first said I would not run, and then announced that I would.

By way of explanation, I told him that I believed running for president was, in truth, my mission, an explanation that Soc also reiterated. Hearing this, you can imagine the incredulous look on his face. Doy was probably thinking, Mission?! What does she think this is? It's an election, not a crusade! As can be expected, nothing came of this meeting.

On December 8, Doy and I met again one final time in his house. Prior to that, I had already heard that he was trying to convince Minnie Osmeña to be his vice-presidential candidate. On this particular night, Doy presented to Soc and me some conditions, which he hoped I would meet in exchange for him giving up the presidency.

First, he said that he wanted the UNIDO to compose one-third of the cabinet. To this, I agreed. Second, he wanted me to run under the UNIDO. I had been asked to run under LABAN, so I told him that I would check on this. Third, he said that in case snap elections were not called, he would be the presidential candidate. I agreed to this as well, because anyway I had said that I would run only if snap elections were called. I agreed also to his condition that he be made prime minister.

But the one condition that I could not accept was that all my appointees should pass his approval first. Even janitors! Perhaps he was thinking that he would agree to be my vice-president, but at the same time also act as co-president or de facto president. And what would I be? I would merely be a symbol, a figurehead.

That night, things were getting very heated between us and I knew that this meeting would be unsuccessful. I left at about two or three in the morning to go back to Times Street and, as I left Doy's house, I in fact saw that they were awaiting the arrival of Minnie Osmeña. I informed Senator Tañada about what Doy and I had discussed, and asked him if it was at all possible for me to run under UNIDO. Senator Tañada, as well as the others, was however firm in the decision that this was impossible. I said that we might have to give in to some of Doy's demands, but that I could not agree to his condition that all my appointees should get his approval first.

In the morning, I gave a press conference stating that Doy and I unfortunately could not come to an agreement, but that I would continue to seek the presidency. I was then asked who my vice-president would be, and I announced that it would be Nene Pimentel.

Then Teng Puyat of Manila Bank called and said that he would like to speak to Doy and me. Teng was one of those people who was very helpful when Ninoy was buried and was also very supportive during the Makati rallies. He talked to both of us, trying to resolve this standoff between Doy and me. He even considered asking us to toss coins or draw lots to see who would be the candidate! Once again, nothing came of this meeting.

On the last day, then, for the filing of certificates of candidacy, I asked Nene to come to Times Street at two in the afternoon. We were to go on a motorcade together to the Commission on Elections (COMELEC) and file our certificates of candidacy. I remember that it was the day of Nene's birthday as well.

That morning, however, I received a call from Joe Concepcion who said that he had talked to Doy and it seemed that there was a chance that Doy would change his mind. Doy was on his way to see Cardinal Sin, and Joe thought that Cardinal Sin might be able to convince Doy, for the country's sake, to run for vice-president instead. He instructed me not to file my certificate of candidacy yet.

Nene arrived in Times at two o'clock in the afternoon. It was his birthday, and he came with all his supporters. I quickly apologized to him and explained that there seemed to be a chance of Doy and me uniting under one ticket. I said that, at the moment, Cardinal Sin was talking to Doy who, it seemed, would finally relent and agree.

I do not blame Nene if he was ready to wring my neck! I had to tell him he was no longer vice-president, and on his birthday at that. But being the gentleman that he is, he assured me that he very well understood the situation.

Also that afternoon, Maur called and said that Speaker Pepito Laurel had suggested that the Aquinos and Laurels get together and meet. We—my mother-in-law, Butz, Peping, Doy, Ambassador Laurel, and others—all went to Maur's house. Speaker Laurel commented that our families have been friends for a very long time and that it should not be very difficult for us to come to an agreement. Peping brought up the issue of me being asked to sign in agreement to the conditions proposed by Doy, to which Speaker Laurel replied that, between friends, there should be no need for that.

I must clarify, therefore, that Doy's allegation in his book that I initialed some document or other is not true. Perhaps he meant the original proposition that I was agreeable to his becoming prime minister. But on that day, the final day for the filing of certificates of candidacy, and coming from Doy's own brother, there was no signing of anything. There was nothing that I signed.

It is good to be underestimated

We had very little money for the campaign in the beginning. It was Doy, actually, who was better prepared in that, being all set to become the presidential candidate, he already had campaign materials at hand. All they had to do was add the word "vice" to his posters and streamers and such. I, on the other hand, had nothing. It wasn't until after two weeks when we had some posters.

It was not until a week or so after Doy and I came to an agreement that contributions for the campaign began to pour in, as the event that the businessmen were waiting for had happened. I thought it unusual that many of my campaign materials, like T-shirts and buttons, were being sold instead of given away. What was even more unusual was that people were eagerly buying them and also contributing freely to the campaign. I say unusual because, when Ninoy ran for the Senate, we had to convince people to wear the T-shirts and put the stickers on their cars. In my case, people were enthusiastically involving themselves in the campaign in however way they could, volunteering their services and even thinking up innovative ways to raise funds. I remember Chino's project, the "*Piso para kay* Cory," where he walked down Ayala Avenue with a grocery cart to ask for donations.

It was a surprise to me, however, to find out that we were spending for everything. I asked Peping why the expenses were not shared equally between Doy and me. He said that that was not the way it was, that it was the presidential candidate who shouldered all expenses. I thought this unfair, though, because I knew for a fact that Doy also received contributions. There were times when I saw him also being handed an envelope, though whether or not we were given the same amount, I do not know. This was just one of the things I learned during the campaign. Every day there was something new to learn.

To prepare myself, I took a crash course on everything from current events and issues to how I should respond to particular questions. Hundreds of questions were prepared, and I was instructed on what I could or could not say. It also helped that I had advisers, like Nene, Monching, Tony Cuenco, Luis Villafuerte, and, of course, the Convenor Group, who would brief me when I appeared before foreign chambers of commerce, the Rotary Club of Manila, and other events that were held here. I was very grateful for this as I did not think that I had to pretend to be knowledgeable in all things, because I was not. There were times, even, when I would readily tell the people that I had brought someone with me who understood the issues better, and refer the question to him.

They subjected me to so many drills! There was one time I was just so tired that nothing was entering my head anymore. If it were the last day of the campaign, it would have been understandable. They could drive me up to the very last minute. But when I thought of all the appearances I still had to make, I felt that I had to conserve my strength.

Oscar Lopez, who is not a doctor, gave me anti-stress pills, which he bought in California. Seven tablets in one package. I don't know why, but I had such trust in him! I did ask Rolly if it was okay and he said it was, so every morning, this was my breakfast. Seven pills. And during the entire sixty-day campaign, the worst illness I got was a sore throat. I never got sick on the campaign trail, though many others had.

A professional, Mark Brown, had also been hired to help me handle interviews, something which I did not relish doing, as I had said many times before. He told me that, for instance, if I were uncomfortable with a particular question, I could evade answering it by saying something else. There were other questions, of course, where he advised me to be very categorical with my answers. Where communism was concerned, I should explicitly say that I will not have anything whatsoever to do with the communists.

My advisers had seen the need to hire Mark as a result of an incident with Seth Mydans, a correspondent for the *New York Times*. Early in the campaign, Lupita thought that I should already meet with the foreign press, although I felt that I was still not prepared to face the media. The *New York Times* people had called to say that they wanted to meet with me, but that it would simply be a social call. That really threw me off, the term "social call." I was too relaxed. And then Seth Mydans came out with this terrible article. In our conversation during that "social call," I had said that I was willing to talk to the communists. He had also asked me if it were possible for someone with communist ideas to be part of my cabinet, and I said yes. Maybe I was ahead of my time! But the article only served to reinforce some people's belief that I was indeed a communist. Luckily, this happened during the first week, or first two weeks, so we were still able to do something about it.

During the campaign, this was the main issue against me. I thought this was the strangest allegation and so simply ignored it. When I went out to the provinces, however, I realized that the people were taking this issue quite seriously. In Mindanao, a nun even asked me why I had not bothered to answer the charge that I was a communist. I asked her if she believed it. She told me that she herself did not, but that many people in Mindanao did because that was all that they had been hearing and I had not refuted it. Because of this, and the article in the *New York Times*, copies of which were plastered all over the walls in Mindanao, I had to categorically deny that I never was a communist and never would be. I told them that I always went to mass, and that my children and I were really very faithful to our religion.

This experience made me very wary of the media, and it was some time before I agreed to be interviewed by the foreign press. I rationalized this by saying that it is not the foreigners who will vote, anyway, so there should be no need to take up time with them. In truth, however, I was afraid that I would make another mistake. As a presidential candidate, I felt a great responsibility not to commit any mistakes, or at least to keep my mistakes to the barest minimum, since so much was dependent on me. This was why the article in the *New York Times* bothered me greatly.

In a way, looking back, it was necessary for me to make that mistake so that I would be humble enough to admit that I needed a lot of expert advice. With that incident with the *New York Times,* I realized my shortcomings and became determined to seek support and assistance. So I had my advisers on specific things, and I had Paul Aquino schedule activities for me, while Peping was the overall head of my campaign. Other things, however, I obviously had to learn on my own as the campaign progressed.

We started each day with a Te Deum, which the bishop of the particular diocese where we were would say for us. Certainly, our starting each day with prayer helped. Everywhere we went, people would approach me and say that they were praying for us. We had tremendous support from the Catholic Church. Cardinal Sin was really most supportive. Many of the nuns and priests were always there for us.

During the sixty-day campaign period, I think, all in all, I visited sixty provinces and gave an average of eight speeches a day, with a record high of fourteen. Sometimes, we would even have something like eight meetings a day. On my birthday, I said that I would take the day off. I wanted to catch up on much-needed sleep and be with my family. But when I think about it, my birthday celebration probably lasted two weeks. Everywhere I went people would be singing "Happy Birthday." Some people even presented me with cakes.

It was very exhausting, and there were times when the places would blur one into the other so that I always had to make sure what province or town we were in. My sister, Terry, helped by writing the names down for me, as I did not want to make a mistake in greeting the people and acknowledging the place where they were from. I also tried to recall the names of all the mayors, until finally we agreed that Doy would be the one to acknowledge the important people who were there. I did not want to take the chance of saying the wrong name, or missing out on somebody's.

My campaign platform centered on the restoration of democracy. I also espoused releasing all political prisoners, retiring all over-staying generals, and calling for a ceasefire with the communist insurgents. The military did not like what I said about releasing political prisoners. But they did like what I said about retiring over-staying generals. This was something that the military had been hoping for, for so long. The call for the ceasefire was first suggested by Homobono Adaza and was meant for the Huks and the NPA.

My speeches also dwelt on the evils inflicted by the Marcos dictatorship, while Doy's dwelt on Ninoy's assassination and pointed to Marcos as the killer, the mastermind. At this point in Doy's speech, the people always loudly cheered and applauded. I touched on this as well, but my style was less straightforward, presenting it in a questioning way. I asked the people how it was possible that anyone could go to the airport tarmac without the consent or knowledge of the military, who were there in the first place on orders of General Ver, who took orders from Marcos, the commander-in-chief.

I also recounted Ninoy's experiences in prison, the sufferings he endured for the sake of his country, culminating in his sacrificing his life because of his great love for the people. I told the people that I was doing what I was doing because I believed that all of us should help in restoring our rights and freedoms, that I was myself ready to offer my life for this cause. Of course, my children were very dismayed by this statement!

It was my first experience in giving speeches for myself and I found it very difficult and uncomfortable to praise myself. I realized, however, that this had to be done if one were trying to sell oneself to the people, if I were to convince the people to believe in me, believe in my cause as passionately as I did.

People also told me that I was too nice in my speeches, that I should be attacking Marcos. Then my nephew, Rapa Lopa, gave me these notes from his dad saying that they realized how averse I was to casting aspersions on the enemy, but that I had to learn to do this. Marcos himself was making all these derogatory statements about me, saying, among other things, that a woman's place was in the bedroom and that I had no experience. This, I countered by saying that certainly I had no experience—unlike him, I had no experience in cheating, lying, stealing, and killing my opponents. This went very well with the crowds. My spokesman, Rene Saguisag, also helped respond to all the things Marcos was saying against me.

Finally we worked it out that Doy would be the more hard-hitting one. I should say that he must be credited with being a very good speaker, with a loud and powerful voice and able to work up the crowds. I learned from watching him and the other politicians deliver their speeches. I realized the reason my speeches were short was that I went straight to the point. My speeches had no flourishes. On the other hand, Doy would repeat things for emphasis. For instance, he would say that I was the widow of Ninoy, and then mention this again. Another thing that he would do was make the observation that the people gathered to see us were packed like sardines so that there was no longer any room to clap. And he would prove his point by asking the crowds to raise their hands in the air and clap. This was a hit with the crowds and they would loudly clap and cheer.

Doy also gave me a very helpful tip with regard to the leis that we were given wherever we went. I had a problem with flowers even then, being allergic to them, and many times the flowers were *calachuchi*, whose fragrance was really very strong. Doy told me that I should simply throw the flowers back to the crowds and they would love it. And they did, reaching out for them and thus relieving me of any allergies that might ensue.

When Ninoy was running for the different political positions, the most I did was shake hands with people in the marketplaces or factories. I never really gave speeches. In time, however, I felt no more nervousness. My speeches came out more naturally. But I was still hesitant to use my arms to gesture, which some people missed seeing. I figured, however, that as a woman candidate I was not expected to be as dramatic or forceful in my gestures as in the case of Doy. Although this whole experience of mine was really most unusual for me, I can now understand the high that one can get when there are all these people clapping wildly even before one has started to speak. It made me feel good, but I also wondered whether or not I deserved all this. Certainly this was something that I never imagined would happen to me.

As the campaign neared its end, Doy and I also included in our speeches an appeal to the people to vote for us and to make sure that their votes were counted. We appealed to them to be vigilant, to guard the ballot boxes, or to volunteer in NAMFREL.

In campaigning, I realized how much more difficult it was for a woman. But I learned to make the best of the situation. I knew that bishops' residences would be the best place to look for a rest room. So maybe this was a second reason I would go see the bishop. Aside from the Te Deum, I also really needed his bathroom facilities! Sometimes we had good food, as when Chito Ayala was our host. But there were times when we had to leave very early in the morning and did not want to bother our hosts about preparing something for us. I do not know how my friend Fritzi Aragon did it, but sometimes we had sandwiches. Most of the time, however, we just had Storck mint candy, which would surprisingly sustain us until evening. I also did not want to eat, anyway, because of the lack of bathroom facilities.

I recall with amusement our stay in Mindanao. We were scheduled to stay for twelve days, but since we were flying in on a light plane, we could only bring a small suitcase. We could not in fact even bring along any food. In my suitcase, I had only three dresses that I was hoping I would be able to wash. It turned out that, instead of "wash and wear," most of the time my clothes would be "wear and wear." Sometimes what Fritzi would do was at least iron the clothes. You can imagine, though, all the perspiration that had soaked into them!

Our most dangerous flight was when we were going to Marawi from Cagayan de Oro. Terry; Eldon, my son-in-law; Nene Pimentel; and I were in a helicopter and had to turn back three times because of the bad weather. We couldn't see anything below us. It was zero visibility, just clouds all around. There was no radar, and the worst thing was we knew we were surrounded by mountains. Finally, we were able to spot a clearing and landed there.

Poor Nene! Imagine, I took back making him my vice-presidential candidate, then had the nerve to ask him later on to accompany me on this Mindanao trip. I had invited him to help me especially with the Moro National Liberation Front (MNLF). Nene, who is from Mindanao, was very knowledgeable about the Muslim problem.

In terms of housing arrangements, Doy always stayed with somebody who was partial to the UNIDO, and I likewise would stay with somebody who was PDP-LABAN or a non-politician. I stayed in all kinds of houses. There was one house where I was waiting for the water from the tap to clear because it was brownish in color. I thought this was because it had earlier rained; but the water stayed brown. So I simply made do with alcohol, water from the refrigerator, and a washcloth. There were times, of course, when there were amenities like air-conditioning. Also, whereas before I used to not be able to sleep on strange beds, during the campaign, regardless of what kind of bed it was, I slept! With or without air-conditioning, it was fine with me.

This was the first time that I had a first-hand experience of what other people's lives were all about. Before, my visits would just be for the day, after which I went back to the comforts and familiarity of my own world. Now I realized how the rest of the country lived. More than that, however, I realized how even in the face of poverty and want the Filipinos are a truly generous lot. It was in these instances when I believed that we had a very good chance of winning. If these people were so willing to part with their hard-earned money, then I was sure that they would be willing not only to vote for us, but to guard the ballot as well.

It was truly amazing, this spontaneous generosity of the people. In Iloilo, as we were driving around town in the rain, a woman rushed up to our jeep and handed Eldon an envelope for me. We presumed it was a letter, but that night when we finally had the chance to open it, Eldon discovered money and a note stating that this was their offering to me. And in a pineapple plantation in Mindanao, as I was speaking before the people there, I noticed them passing around a plastic bucket. This puzzled me until, at the end, they came up to me and gave me, together with baskets of pineapples and bananas, the plastic bucket—and in it were pesos and coins for me.

I knew that these people needed the money more than I did. But at the same time I always remembered what Ninoy said, that when the poor offered one something, one should never say no. This would only hurt their feelings. The poor know how incapable they are of giving something truly worthwhile, but just the same they want to give something of themselves.

I think it was Lupita who told me that I had finally made it with the crowds because everybody was just wanting to touch me, to be as close to me as possible. This was a Filipino habit, which indicated that they liked me.

It sometimes led, however, to quite awkward situations as when the people would touch our legs as we went up the stage! I was also always reminded never to extend my hands out to the people because they will pull on them, and I could hurt myself that way. Despite an inner shield of relatives and friends around me and an outer shield of men around them, I would still feel these aches and pains at the end of the day.

Everywhere we went, crowds of people would show up, a source of amazement to me. Even while driving down the highways, I would see all these people lined up all along the way. They would wave anything yellow, yellow bananas or papaya leaves, yellow curtains, and even, once, a yellow half-slip! It was unbelievable how masses of them would show up on their own volition. I don't think you'll be seeing crowds like those again, who were not only eager to see you, but were also willing to spend time and money.

My security would always make sure that every place we visited was safe. But it was really the people who made me feel safe. They made me feel not only very hopeful, but also safe, that they would not let any harm come upon us, even when we ventured into areas where they were very much affected by the communist insurgency.

We had been warned about the dangers of going into these areas, actually been discouraged from going, but I guess it really was incumbent upon us to try to visit as many places as possible. People were telling us to be careful, and, in fact, we did have some tension-filled moments in Basilan. When we entered the town, one of the leaders there told me that he saw a sign saying *"Isang bala ka lang,* Cory." (It will only take one bullet.) It was quite unnerving to see so many people carrying Armalite rifles. Still, the people eagerly received us. As part of my speech, I told the crowds that I had seen the sign. I told them my answer to that was, *"Isang balota ka lang,* Marcos!" (You will only have one ballot.)

Marcos, at this time, could no longer go to the places I was going to because he was very ill. Towards the end, during their *miting ɩe avance,* he even had to be carried up on stage. Normally this is done as a sign of approaching victory and his handlers made it appear so. In truth, it was because he would not have been able to make it up the stage on his own.

Eventually, I suppose I became adjusted to my role as presidential candidate. I do not think I totally enjoyed it the way Ninoy would have. Many times, I thought about how he would have loved every minute of what I was going through. But then he had to die. If I died, I don't think it would have made a difference!

For me, as I said, seeking the presidency was a mission, and my concern was to do the best I could. At the beginning of each day, I would pray to God and ask for His help, pray that everything would turn out all right. And while I had been thinking of whom I would ask to be members of the cabinet (I had always had in mind Jimmy, Nene, and some other politicians who were helping, like Neptali Gonzales), in truth, I did not think very much beyond what if I won or lost. I think the people around me were also that way. Our focus was not what kind of government we were going to have. Our focus was getting Marcos out. This by itself was already a formidable task, and to succeed in it would have already been a tremendous accomplishment. People must have thought I was being overly optimistic. But we all presumed there would be a transition period, anyway. Who could have known then that there would be none?

Many of these politicians, in fairness to them, were sincere in their support for me. Among them, the one who truly believed in me was Senator Tañada. Some, however, were, I felt, rather resentful. I know they did not deem me capable since they felt that I did not know anything and that they were better than me. I always felt that Jovy, every time he would see me when I was already president, could not accept that somebody "lesser" than him was president. I felt this way about Doy as well, that he was thinking that it should be him in my place. It would do well to remind these people that none of this was my own doing.

I was also thinking that some of these politicians, or some of the would-be presidentiables, agreed to give way to me only because they believed defeating Marcos was anyway a losing proposition. Giving way to me was ostensibly an act of *noblesse oblige*, but I think these politicians were also fearful of going up against Marcos. The people had wanted to fight with Ninoy's last drop of blood, and Ninoy did. Since Ninoy was gone, people probably figured that I could take his place. But they were also perhaps thinking that if I indeed became president they would end up calling the shots just the same because of my lack of experience. Slowly, however, they realized that I was my own person and that I had a mind of my own.

Sometimes, it is good to be underestimated.

It was now or never

Before Election Day, people in charge of my security had advised me to lie low after I vote because it was important that I stay alive. I voted in Tarlac, after which my family and I came back to Manila.

The first two days, I remained out of sight, hardly stepping out of the Zobels' condominium in Makati where we were staying, only doing so to meet with people in the office at Jose Cojuangco and Sons building in Legazpi Village, Makati. But on the third day, I felt that it was time I go out and be seen. I went to the Makati Municipal Hall and there encountered people who asked me what they could do, because they knew that Marcos was already manipulating the election returns.

We expected this, of course. There was no way he was going to concede victory to me, the wife of Ninoy. In fact, two or three weeks before the elections, Peping and I met with Joe Almonte, who was a colonel then, and he told me matter-of-factly that there was no way that I could win. As early as then, he said, they were already preparing the ballots in the military camps. Even in Makati, which that time was controlled by Mayor Nemesio Yabut, his people had already stuffed the ballot boxes so full that, come Election Day, no more ballots could be put in. It was on this occasion, I recall, that Almonte also mentioned that the only way to oust Marcos was through a coup d'etat. He further suggested that we forego the elections and join forces with them, the military. But I told him that I wasn't in it for the power. I just really wanted to know, not only what the Filipino people thought of me, but also whether or not they really wanted a change in the system.

It wasn't just Almonte who felt that it was a losing cause, that no way could I win. Even the foreign correspondents thought the same thing. They thought, sure, I was popular, but they will never read the votes in my favor. I guess those who were privy to the hard realities of elections under a dictator were so sure that I could not win.

All over the country, there was rampant cheating in Marcos's favor. The teachers, in charge of the polling areas and of counting the ballots, were coerced to cheat. In my home province of Tarlac, people were harassed, beaten, and, worse, killed. One of the victims was a close supporter—I was a sponsor at his wedding—who was shot and killed in Capas, Tarlac. His killers even severed his thumb and forefinger, so that he would never be able to make the L sign for LABAN again. It was very gruesome and clearly a warning to all my supporters that they could end up the same way.

On February 11, Evelio Javier, one of my most loyal supporters, was also gunned down in Antique trying to safeguard the ballots. His body was brought to Manila, then laid in state in Baclaran Church and the Ateneo, where thousands of people came to pay their respects and show their solidarity. People were very dismayed by this event. So you can see why the people wanted to do something about the continuing abuses of the Marcos regime.

There were other acts of bravery and defiance. One incident (one in a chain of events that would lead to the ouster of the dictator) that caused quite a stir among the people was when a group of computer operators staged a walk-out, after finding discrepancies in the election returns they were tabulating for the COMELEC. During these snap elections, the COMELEC was headed by Leonie Perez who, even during the LABAN campaign, masterminded the cheating. These computer operators had to go into hiding, and some of them had to be sheltered in Baclaran Church and the Ateneo. I think Cardinal Sin also helped them.

During the elections, there were a number of foreign correspondents as well as foreign observers. After, CBS, an American news network, remarked that I must have won by such a wide margin because even up to the last day Marcos was still cheating me. The way he did it was the results would not come in at the same time. The results from Isabela, for instance, were held back until the very last moment. Enrile himself admitted that in his region alone, Region II under which Isabela belongs, I was cheated out of 350,000 votes. Imagine that number subtracted from my votes and added on to Marcos's. So right there and then that was 700,000 votes for Marcos.

At this time, US president Ronald Reagan issued a statement that both sides had cheated in the elections. Hearing this infuriated me. I knew that he had still to read the report of Sen. Richard Lugar, head of the US observers, who had not even returned to Washington and submitted his report. It was no secret that Marcos and Reagan were very close. In fact, it was later revealed that Marcos could not understand why it seemed that Reagan was abandoning him, when he had even donated $10 million to Reagan's campaign.

The US ambassador, Steve Bosworth, wanted to see me to explain Reagan's statement. I was in no mood to see him, but Peping and Monching prevailed upon me. Ambassador Bosworth apologized and said that President Reagan was probably misinformed and that the issue would be corrected in the next few days. Ambassador Bosworth would later tell people that I received him very coldly.

Once Senator Lugar and company returned to Washington, they submitted a full report that stated very categorically that there was rampant cheating by the Marcos camp, of which they had documented evidence. The report also stated that I had, indeed, won.

The cheating was so brazen, the Filipino people felt that they had to finally do something to get rid of the dictator. It was now or never. There was an air of restiveness, a pressing for action.

Three or four days after the elections, during a meeting with the opposition leaders, I asked to call for a rally. Neptali told me that rallies are no longer called after an election, more so if the candidate lost. But I asked that I be given this one chance because people were clamoring to do something more. I said that I would like to hold the rally at the Luneta. They told me, however, that Liwasang Bonifacio would be a more manageable venue. It was smaller, and a crowd of twenty thousand people would already look substantial. I, however, insisted on holding it at the Luneta, the biggest open space possible. I wanted to find out once and for all if the people were still willing to continue the fight for our democracy and do something about the manipulated election results.

Doy was not at this meeting, but he had a representative there. When he found out about my plans, he was very angry because he felt that I should have consulted him. I told him that his representative was present at the meeting and therefore knew about it and should have informed him. He was very upset and warned me that if no one showed up it would be extremely embarrassing. I told him that he did not have to go if he did not want to, that it was all right by me.

I myself also did not know what to expect. But on February 16, the day of the rally, the Luneta was a sea of people. This was the day after Marcos was declared the winner by the parliament. This was also the day the Catholic Bishops Conference of the Philippines (CBCP) issued a pastoral letter, where they said that the Filipino people were under no obligation to recognize the winner of a very fraudulent election. The CBCP was in fact supporting my non-violent protest movement that I announced during the Luneta rally.

In planning for this non-violent protest movement, someone initially suggested that the people be asked not to pay their taxes. Someone else, however, disagreed and pointed out to me that if I became president, I might have a difficult time asking people to pay their taxes. I want it on record, therefore, that I never asked for the non-payment of taxes.

What I asked for was the removal of bank deposits from banks owned by Marcos or his cronies, and I mentioned the banks involved. I also said that the people should not purchase the products of known Marcos cronies. I also mentioned the newspapers, owned by Marcos cronies, that they were to boycott.

Some people in the opposition thought these inadequate and would not lead to Marcos's ouster. My thinking, however, was to begin with small deeds, to see first if the people would do these small things before asking them to do bigger things.

It was at this time that Philip Habib, a special envoy of Pres. Ronald Reagan, came to Manila. I was told that he came to specifically ask me to accept a position in the Marcos government. I asked an American friend, whom I thought might be able to relay the message to Habib, to tell him that if that was his purpose in coming then he was simply wasting his time, and mine. By chance, however, he had been billeted at the Manila Hotel right across Luneta and arrived a day after the rally. I suppose, therefore, that he had an inkling of what the real situation was, the real sentiment of the people.

When he finally saw me, he apologized and quickly explained that I must have gotten the wrong message. It was never his intention, he said, to ask me to be part of the Marcos government. He merely wanted to know what the opposition was planning to do next. (I thought, What a politician he is!) He also wanted to know how long we thought we could keep up the protest movement. I told him six months. Of course, that was an exaggeration, as we did not have the finances for a long, drawn-out protest. I thought three months was a more realistic period because, aside from the financial constraints, people might begin to lose interest. At that time, neither of us thought that the end would come in just a matter of days.

To make the people aware of this non-violent protest movement, I had planned to go to ten cities or ten towns throughout the Philippines. I went first to Angeles in Pampanga, and then Cebu.

A coup plot uncovered

The day before I was to leave for Cebu, on February 21, Lt. Angel Honrado warned me that he had heard rumors of a coup and advised me not to leave for Cebu. But I had heard such rumors so often, and they never came true. If the coup attempt did not happen, what then? I told him that if I did not go to Cebu, nothing might come of my non-violent protest movement. Also, the people there were expecting me and had prepared for my coming.

Lieutenant Honrado would not give up and went to see Peping to ask him to dissuade me from going. But Peping told him that once I had made up my mind, it was difficult to convince me otherwise. Other opposition leaders, like Nene, Monching, John Osmeña, and Tony Cuenco, had planned to accompany me to Cebu.

The rally in Cebu that Saturday, February 22, was held in the afternoon. Then, at about six in the evening, the columnist Belinda Cunanan told me some stunning news. She had just talked to Eggie Apostol, publisher of *Mr. and Ms. Magazine* and *Philippine Daily Inquirer*, who told her that Enrile and Eddie Ramos were holed up in Camp Aguinaldo, where they had taken refuge to escape from Marcos. Marcos had discovered that there was a coup plot against him. General Ver then arrested one or two of the supposed conspirators, who confessed on television that they, together with Enrile and the Reform the Armed Forces Movement (RAM), were going to stage the coup. Enrile and Eddie Ramos had been found out and had to flee to Camp Aguinaldo. (There, Enrile later confessed on television that the ambush attempt on him, which Marcos had used to justify martial law, had been staged and that Marcos was in on it.)

I could not believe it at first, until we verified the news. Then I was able to talk to Enrile about two hours later. I asked him how he was and he sounded very nervous. I told him that there was not much I could do except pray for him, and he said that they certainly were in need of prayers. Butz was apparently one of the first to give his support to Enrile and Ramos and had asked the members of ATOM to go to Camp Aguinaldo to show their support for them.

I was staying with the Quisumbings in Cebu, and I was told that I should move elsewhere because Marcos and his men knew I was there. Monching said that the American Embassy had a Navy boat docked in the area and thought that I could ask the consul general if I could seek shelter there. The American consul general did invite me, but I declined.

I decided that I would go to the Carmelite Convent, instead, where I could pray and the nuns could pray for us as well. Because we had to move in secret, I asked Tony Cuenco to drive for us. I also asked Nancy, his wife, to lend me a dress because I only had a yellow one, which would make me look very conspicuous.

Kris and I, together with Tony, Nancy, and Peping, proceeded to the convent. When we got there, the nuns reassuringly told me not to worry because the Marcos forces would have to kill them first before they would allow them to get to us. It did feel very much like we were in *The Sound of Music!*

The nuns told me this was the first time they allowed men to enter and even sleep in the convent, although I doubt very much if Peping and Tony were able to sleep at all. I, at least, was able to get two or three hours of restful sleep. When I went down at about six in the morning, Monching and the others were already there. Apparently, they had been banging on the gates since very early in the morning. But the nuns, true to their word, did not let them in, thinking they might be the enemy!

Monching suggested that from Cebu I fly to Palawan and then to Malaysia. They were thinking that it would be safer for me to bide my time there and then come back to Manila later. I was thinking, what would I do there? Besides, I said, Marcos at this time was certainly more preoccupied with Enrile and Ramos than with me. So I opted to go back to Manila.

Before I left on Sunday, February 23, we organized a press conference, aired by Radio Veritas and other local stations, where I issued a statement saying that I was in support of Enrile and Ramos. This was because, at that time, we in the opposition went by the saying "The enemy of my enemy is my friend." This was a unifying factor then, and there was also the fact that the RAM themselves had stated they were out to seek reforms. Moreover, we realized, that for us to succeed, we would need the military's cooperation and support. I had actually met members of RAM during the campaign. My sister-in-law, Mila Albert, was the widow of Charlie Albert, a captain in the Philippine Navy, who knew some of them. They had asked to meet with me. They asked me about my security, and so I told them that I had people from Tarlac handling it. In one of my earlier speeches also (in October 1985 in Singapore, during the Country Risk Seminar on the Philippines to which Bernie Villegas and Jimmy invited me), while I categorically stated that while it was true that some of the military were responsible for the assassination of my husband, I was not prepared to condemn the entire organization for the sins of a few.

In the same press conference, I also asked the people to go to EDSA and lend their support as well. I then thanked those in government who had resigned their positions and had openly declared their support for Enrile and Ramos. We had heard that many of them, like Roilo Golez and Justice Claudio Teehankee, who were among the first, had renounced their support for Marcos.

For our flight to Manila, the first suggestion was for us to take the Philippine Airlines flight. However, as Nancy found out, all the flights were already fully booked. Then Bea Zobel very generously called for her plane to pick me up in Cebu and fly me home. We discovered, however, that someone had diverted the flight, taken the plane to fly somewhere else! I realized that in very critical and dangerous moments, one can really tell who are courageous and who are not. Finally, we were able to fly back using the same light plane that we took going to Cebu. It was important that no one knew of our plans or whereabouts, as our safety was at risk, and it was fortunate that the tower in the Cebu airport never reported that we had taken off.

In Manila, not very many people were aware that I had already gotten back. From the airport to my sister's house in Wack Wack, where we had decided to stay, we were travelling on EDSA right beside the tanks and trucks carrying military personnel. On orders of Marcos, these had been massing on EDSA, near Camp Aguinaldo, to quell whatever support there was for Enrile and Ramos. People had been coming in droves, peacefully and quietly gathering on EDSA as they heeded our call for support, including Cardinal Sin's.

No one, however, knew I was inside the car, as it was heavily tinted. It was only CNN that got wind of my arrival, but those people who could get connected to Clark Airbase were able to watch on their television screens our arrival in my sister's house. It turned out to be no big secret after all!

It was in my sister's house where I met with the leaders of the opposition. I suppose it was that Sunday night that I met with Doy, who told me that there was a recommendation that we form a civil-military junta, until elections could be called. Enrile and Ramos would of course be part of it, as well as Doy and me, and I think either Celing Muñoz-Palma or Senator Tañada. My first reaction was skepticism. What was that all about? I couldn't believe that Doy seemed amenable to that proposal. I was not in favor of such a thing.

I also met separately with Enrile and Ramos. When I met with Enrile, it was so strained. In fairness to him, however, I suppose it was just me. Although it was Marcos, not him, who was responsible for the detention of Ninoy, he was still the person I had to ask for so-called privileges in the matter of Ninoy's detention, and he seemed to me a little intimidating still. It was different with Ramos. I felt it was easier to talk to him. I suppose it was because I never had any real dealings with him in the past.

I had also talked to Rocky Ileto, someone many of us felt could be trusted, and told him that I would like to have his help. He said, however, that he had already been asked by Enrile to be his deputy minister, but that he would still be able to help in that capacity.

People had told me that, initially, that Saturday and Sunday, Enrile kept mentioning my name and making the LABAN sign. Then that Monday, February 24, he had stopped doing so; people were no longer hearing my name. I remember it was Mon del Rosario and Joker Arroyo who said that I should take my oath of office right away. Enrile was no longer mentioning my name, and they felt that he must have other plans.

We met with the leaders of the opposition—Senator Tañada, Jovy, Pepe, Celing—in my sister's house, and they all agreed that I should take my oath of office that very day. Doy was informed, and we decided that we would hold it at the Club Filipino. For this, however, a new oath had to be drafted, because to whom would I pledge? We did not recognize the 1973 Constitution, and so the lawyers present decided that I would pledge to defend and preserve the fundamental law.

I also insisted to Peping that I would go to EDSA. Peping disapproved of my going there because if I got killed, he said, it would be the end of everything, not just for me, but for all the people there who were hoping for a change. He argued that I was anyway in constant touch with the people through the radio stations and they very well knew that I was one with them.

I felt, however, that it was unfair of me to tell them to go to EDSA and put them at risk. I must also be willing to do the same. Besides, I had already announced that I was going to be there on Monday. I asked Peping to see to my security and informed him that at four o'clock, with or without the security, I was going. He was very upset. When it came to my children, though, he put his foot down and told them that they could not come. Noynoy went, but the girls had to stay.

They were able to find a good spot for me at the POEA building. From there, I saw for myself the masses of people who, during the last two days and nights, had peacefully gathered on EDSA, clutching rosaries and holding images of the Virgin Mary, singing inspiring songs and always praying. Many of the people there were priests, seminarians, and nuns. They had stopped the tanks and the trucks in their paths and prevented them from reaching Camps Crame and Aguinaldo, where Enrile and Ramos and their men continued to be holed up. They cheered when they heard news of officers and soldiers defying the orders of General Ver and defecting to our side.

I stayed for some fifteen minutes at the POEA, where I joined the crowd in singing the "Our Father." I just wanted to show the people that I was still with them. I told them that for the first time in history the civilians were called upon to protect the military. I also thanked them for their courage, their conviction, and support, then headed back to Wack Wack.

It took awhile for my oath to be finalized and when it was done, it was already getting dark. I suggested then that we postpone the oath-taking ceremony for the next day. I did not want people to risk their lives going to Club Filipino for the oath-taking ceremony, in case the Marcos forces took advantage of the dark to do something. That was how Marcos and I came to take our oaths of office on the same day, Tuesday, February 25.

The People Power president

Tuesday morning, Father Bernas, Father Arevalo, Fr. Guido Arguelles, and Jimmy Ongpin came to my house, together with two generals. The generals were trying to convince me to change the venue of the oath-taking ceremony. They thought they would be able to provide me with better security in Crame. I felt, however, that it would be best to have it in a civilian venue and told them that I had already announced it would be in Club Filipino. Besides, I reasoned, it would be difficult to get to Crame considering the huge crowds gathered there. The generals told me that they could make arrangements for me to be flown there by helicopter. But, no, I did not want that and declined.

Later on, Father Bernas took me aside and told me that the generals were upset because it seemed that I did not trust them, in spite of all that they had risked for me. It was not a question of trust, I said, but of practicality. We had already made preparations in Club Filipino and the people had already been informed the oath-taking ceremony would be held there.

While I was getting dressed, I heard the sound of gunfire. Shooting had broken out in Channel 9, one of the television stations near our house. I think it was an encounter between remnants of the forces still supportive of the Marcos administration and the soldiers that had turned over to our side. That was very alarming, although I remember Jimmy trying to ease the tension by telling me not to worry because he and his son, Apa, who was also there, would act as my bulletproof shields.

From my house in Times Street, I went to my sister's house in Wack Wack and from there proceeded to Club Filipino. An overflowing crowd had assembled there. Teddy Boy Locsin told me that I was, apparently, expected to read from a prepared speech, and so he wrote a brief message on the back of a telegram and a paper napkin and handed these to me. For the rest of the speech, I simply extemporized, saying that we should all reconcile for the good of the Filipino people. I also had to give a salute, a very awkward one because it was my first time to do so. Ramos took me by surprise—I did not think he was going to give me a salute—so I appeared very hesitant and the newspapers made such a fuss over that.

All in all, it was a very singular and unique oath-taking ceremony because, when I took my oath of office, the de facto president was still Marcos, who was still in Malacañang.

After Club Filipino, I said that I wanted to go to Manila Memorial Park to visit Ninoy's tomb. Jojo Binay had to arrange for us to get through the barricades of trucks and such that had been set up on EDSA. When we got to Manila Memorial Park, my children and I prayed at Ninoy's tomb. I was thinking, well, Ninoy, what now?

That afternoon, Ambassador Bosworth called. He told me that they were trying to work through Marcos's sons-in-law, Tommy Manotoc and Greggy Araneta, to try to convince him to leave the country. Marcos was in very poor physical condition. He could no longer make correct judgments and be on top of the situation as he was once able to do. Still, the thought of letting go of all their wealth and power was something the Marcoses could not fathom. They did not want to admit that their moment of truth had come. I had heard that, in those four days that would come to be known as the People Power Revolution, a rocket had been fired towards Malacañang and that it had hit the car of one of the sons-in-law. For the first time in their lives, I suppose, the Marcoses felt a very real and immediate threat to their lives. So while it was difficult to give up all that they had, they were terrified for their lives and wanted to escape.

(I remember the December 1989 coup attempt, when I was already president. At the height of it, and thinking that my life could be very soon ended, I thought about which of my things I would save. I called

Fr. Bobby Perez of San Beda and gave him Ninoy's and my diaries for safekeeping. The thought also crossed my mind that if I died, then at least it was for the people. I had also sent all the househelp away. I thought, why make everybody die with us? So it was just Noynoy, Viel, Kris, and me. Ballsy and Pinky were already married and living elsewhere. We, of course, prayed; and I reassured them that whatever happened God would take care of us. We could hear the exchange of firepower. I even heard on the radio someone on our side warning the others not to waste bullets because they might run out of them.)

That evening, Ambassador Bosworth called to say that the Marcoses had finally left Malacañang, and that they were on their way to the embassy enroute to Clark. Before they reached Clark, Ambassador Bosworth called again and said that Marcos was asking if they could go to Paoay, in Ilocos, instead. I asked if he was in danger of dying, because, if he were, I thought I should let the man die in his own country. Ambassador Bosworth however said that Marcos was not in danger of dying, only very tired. In that case, I said, let him spend the night in Clark, but the following morning he must go.

Later, when the Marcoses had reached Honolulu, it was discovered that Marcos had brought with him P27 million in cash. Imagine what he could have done with that sum! I guess he was really wanting to go to Paoay so he could gather his loyal troops and retake Malacañang.

The night the Marcoses left, there were such joyous celebrations in the streets.

And at nine o'clock that evening of February 25, I guess I became president.

I slept in Roberts Street in Pasay that night, in the house of my sister, Terry, and returned to Times Street the next day. I was trying to form my cabinet. I appointed Joker executive secretary. I told Jimmy that he would be minister of finance. He refused at first, saying that he did not want any position. I told him, however, that he had gotten me into this, therefore he had no choice but to accept it. The other members, among others, were Neptali as minister of justice, Enrile as minister of defense, Ramos as chief of staff, and Nene as minister of local government. On the matter of the RAM, Chito Ayala helped me develop closer ties with the military.

My personal choice to head the Presidential Security Group was Col. Voltaire Gazmin. It was providential that, when I was campaigning in Iligan, he sent me a calling card through somebody and said that, if ever I needed security, to call him. So when I became president and was looking for somebody, his name was still fresh in my mind and so I called him. Again, I attribute this to Divine Providence. Why did he again resurrect in my life after all those years? The last time I saw him was in Fort Magsaysay. But this was one of the wisest decisions I have ever made. He was not only loyal, but also very competent. He was really able to protect me and protect the country the whole six years and four months I was president.

I had to give a press conference the very next day to announce my cabinet. I held this at the Mondragon Building as I could not yet go to Malacañang. My head of security told me that they still had to clean up the place and borrow dogs from the American Embassy to sniff out explosives. It turned out that there *were* explosives, buried in the grounds of Malacañang by Marcos's loyal followers. I suppose before the Marcoses left, their people planted these explosives so that, in case the people stormed Malacañang, they would encounter these buried explosives.

So there I was, from housewife to president, the highest position in the land. I suppose it was all providential. If Ver had not discovered the coup plot, there would be no reason for Enrile and Ramos to go hiding in Camp Aguinaldo. But if I had not participated in the elections, what would they be protesting about? Everything just fell into place. I would say that all this was wrought by prayer and that it was through the people's sacrifices that God came to our rescue and did things in a very peaceful way. Suppose, also, that Marcos had let me win. I don't think I would have lasted because he would still be controlling the Batasan and could very well arrange for me to be impeached. He would also still be in control of the military.

My adversaries would say that I was not the winner because I was not proclaimed by the Batasan, and therefore anyone had the right to the presidency. I always go back to the fact, however, that I was the candidate, I did participate in the elections, and I did win—except that I was cheated. I was the one who filed a certificate of candidacy and sought the mandate of the people. That is the important difference.

Let's just say that we need different leaders for different times. The people thought I was the only one who could unite the opposition, who had a chance. They felt they needed someone who was the complete opposite of Marcos. They believed that someone was me.

EPILOGUE
by Rapa Lopa

I began putting this book together immediately after the May 2019 midterm elections. While doing so, I could not help but relate the volatile times we are currently living in to the uncertain and trying times that served as the backdrop of Auntie Cory's stories.

Feeling much frustration and disappointment, I asked myself why, after all these years, a majority of our people seem to be once again accepting of the re-emergence of an oppressive and repressive authoritarian regime. Why, despite the thousands of extra-judicial killings, do the majority of our people seem to be inured to these, seem to suffer from apathy and indifference? Worse, there are those who even condone these killings.

It is also disturbing to note how the majority of our people appear to have grown tolerant of the various high-profile cases of corruption involving our government officials.

Then I recalled one of our early Aquino Foundation meetings with Auntie Cory in March 2007. Our discussions had veered toward what was happening in the country at that time, when we were again experiencing political instability amid corruption allegations and a questionable mandate raised against then-president Gloria Macapagal-Arroyo.

In that meeting, feeling doubtful about any hope for our country, we had asked Auntie Cory, "*May pag-asa pa ba ang bayan natin?*" (Is there still hope for our country?)

She had immediately replied, "*Hoy, kayo ha! Bawal mawalan ng pag-asa. Habang buhay kayo, hindi pwedeng tumigil lumaban para sa tama!*" (One must never lose hope! Until your last breath, you must always fight for what is right!)

We had fallen silent. Then she had continued, very casually, "*Baka dapat may mamatay.*" (Maybe someone should die.)

What had followed was nervous laughter. Taken aback by this statement, we had tried to make light of it by pointing to each other. Who among us would be willing to make the ultimate sacrifice in the same way Uncle Ninoy did on August 21, 1983? Of course, we all knew that our non-heroic lives, even if we offered them, would not have pushed our people to defiant action.

When Auntie Cory said this, she perhaps believed that no less than another heroic act could again collectively inspire our people, moving them to unite for change.

The only question was: Whose life would it be?

Fast forward to February 25, 2008. I had accompanied her to a Makati Business Club meeting where she was invited to speak on the occasion of the twenty-second anniversary of the 1986 People Power Revolution. As she spoke, I noticed that she was gasping for air each time she read the longer sentences of her prepared speech. On our way back to the office, I asked her if she had been having difficulty breathing while delivering her speech. "Yes," she admitted, and self-diagnosed that it must be her asthma acting up again.

A few weeks later, Ate Ballsy called and told me, "Kuys, bad news! Mom has cancer!" I was shocked. It was the kind of news you hope you'd never receive.

The next day, I got a short text message from Auntie Cory: Please come to the office. There, she told me, "I just want you to know I have cancer.

Do not worry about me. I am at peace. I feel I have lived a full life *naman*."

Honestly, I did not know how to react. Even if Ate Ballsy had already informed me that Auntie Cory had cancer, it still felt surreal hearing it directly from her. A part of me still did not want to believe the diagnosis, did not want to accept that Auntie Cory was going to have to go through yet another very grueling battle, this time with a considerable chance she would lose and leave us.

True enough, in June 2009, after a year and two months of treatment, Ate Ballsy shared with me the sad news that Auntie Cory's cancer cells were no longer being neutralized by chemotherapy and the other interventions tried by her doctors.

Auntie Cory had lost her appetite and was no longer eating enough, so that she had lost so much weight and was very pale and weak. I remember Dr. Alex Ayco going to the office with a nurse, who brought with her a bottle of dextrose, so that Auntie Cory could at least be given some nourishment intravenously.

In her yellow conference room, Ate Ballsy and I took turns keeping Auntie Cory company as she settled herself on a recliner, chatting about various topics to preoccupy ourselves.

In one moment of silence, Auntie Cory suddenly remarked, "I thought there was going to be more time." Then she rested her cheek on her hand, closed her eyes, and fell asleep.

Amid the ensuing silence, I saw a very weary woman who, only a few months before, was still attending prayer gatherings and street rallies to protest corruption in the Arroyo administration. I saw the mother of Philippine Democracy—who once led the resistance that ended the reign of tyranny and oppression under a dictator—literally shrinking.

As I remember that day, I cannot help but think what she meant by having or wanting "more time." Clearly, something in her had changed in the period between her cancer diagnosis in March 2008, when she was at peace with the thought of dying after having lived a full life, and this moment, when she seemed wistful about life slipping away too soon.

I can only surmise that she may have been struggling with certain unanswered questions in her mind.

Could she have been asking herself if she had already truly fulfilled her promise to Uncle Ninoy to achieve the goals he'd set out to complete? In fact, one time, I remember she remarked, partly in jest, "*Itong si* Ninoy, *ah! Ang mga sakripisyo ko para sa mga hindi niya natapos,* beyond 'death do us part' *na!*" (Oh, this Ninoy! All these sacrifices I am making for his unfinished mission are already beyond my marriage vows of 'till death do us part'!)

At the same time, considering the huge responsibility thrust upon her shoulders when she became president, was she also pondering if she had actually done enough for their children? She expected, from the very beginning of her married life with Uncle Ninoy, that her role would be limited to that of dutiful wife and nurturing mother. But as we all know, and as fate and destiny would have it, her calling as a mother extended far beyond nurturing her five children to encompass caring for a whole country.

Having embraced this expanded role, as president and public servant, was she also thinking of what she still wanted or needed to accomplish for the country, given the ominous political events that were taking place at the time? Was she still hoping that she would regain her strength and continue her mission of leaving her country a better place for the next generation of Filipinos? Could she also have been contemplating, with both contentment and regret, some of the more difficult choices and decisions she had made in her life? Did she agonize over the uncertainty of not knowing whether all her sacrifices actually amounted to any change in the lives of the people she had devoted her life to?

I like to suppose that, during that somber afternoon in June 2009, some forty days before her death, as the dextrose fluids slowly dripped into her arm, Auntie Cory may have tried to find comfort and consolation in looking back on the past, on the life she had led.

As I write this, I am imagining myself back with Auntie Cory in that yellow conference room, where most of these anecdotes of the pivotal, thirteen-year period of her life with Uncle Ninoy were first verbalized through intimate conversations and interviews. I recall her gestures, her voice. And I am moved to express to her how her story has so resonated with me, helping me come to some realizations and valuable lessons culled from her life's journey. Given one more chance to be back in that yellow room, I picture myself telling her:

Saying yes to love

Sometimes I wonder. Had you known that, by saying yes to Uncle Ninoy's proposal of marriage and what would turn out to be a life of so many trials and sufferings, would you have had second thoughts? Still, I know from how your life unfolded that you had no regrets, as you chose to embrace the unexpected twists and turns of your life with Uncle Ninoy and the hardships and struggles that came with it. And I continue to be awed by your unquestionable support for the cause that Uncle Ninoy had taken on and how you wholly surrendered yourself to it.

From your and Uncle Ninoy's example, I see that saying yes to the invitation to love demands continuous self-giving and sacrifice.

I know Uncle Ninoy could have simply chosen to play transactional politics with the dictator and navigate his way towards his lifelong dream of being president. But he refused this track and chose to remain in jail for seven years and seven months. He could have also chosen to remain in exile in Boston, where you were blessed with the happiest years of your family life. After all, he was even being dissuaded from coming home by the Marcos administration with warnings of an alleged assassination plot against him. Yet, he chose to go home and, despite your fears, you knew in your heart how his deep love for our country and people would eclipse any thought of possible danger or risk.

His coming home, ending tragically as it did, truly sparked something in the hearts of our people. I must admit that I never expected the magnitude of love and sympathy that our people expressed for Uncle Ninoy in the aftermath of his assassination. Hundreds of thousands had gathered at his funeral to reciprocate his ultimate act of love, to show him, in turn, their love for him.

In your case, I know that your only desire was to be the perfect wife to Uncle Ninoy and mother to Ate Ballsy, Pinky, Noy, Viel, and Kris. But when you chose to be the wife of a very dynamic, charismatic, and driven politician, you accepted early on that Uncle Ninoy's time with you and your children would be secondary to his time spent with the constituents he had chosen to serve. This meant that the critical role of parenting would fall mostly on you. It also meant giving up your valued privacy, since Uncle Ninoy literally opened the doors of your home to people from all walks of life.

As it also turned out, the calling to be a dutiful wife and virtually a single parent became a more real challenge when you became the political detainee's wife and the widow of a fallen opposition leader; then the reluctant candidate, who challenged the dictator; and eventually the president of a very wounded people and a country left in ruins.

It was another invitation to love.

And, although I know that you had the option of simply staying in your comfort zone—the temptation to do so is very human—you, and Uncle Ninoy when he was alive, time and again did the exact opposite.

You said yes to the invitation to show your love for our country and people, to continue the struggle and win back our freedom from the repression and oppression of the dictatorship.

Struggles, setbacks, and failures are all grace

Seeing the current state of our country, I struggle with the thought that we, who have pursued the democratic way, may not have done enough to better the lives of our marginalized countrymen and women. I ask myself if the majority of our people have already given up on democracy. Have they reached a point of helplessness and hopelessness so that they are again willing to embrace the patronage of the dictatorship of the few who yield economic and political power? Are the gains of our struggle to bring back freedom and strengthen our democracy for the benefit of all Filipinos already irrelevant?

I sometimes feel overwhelmed by what seems like a never-ending battle to uplift the vast majority of our people who remain poor and vulnerable to the patronage culture that we as a country can't seem to shake off.

I realize that it can be very daunting and frustrating to fight battles that are much larger than us. Setbacks and failures can mercilessly pull us down and intimidate us into submission. There is also the pain of persecution from people who oppose our views and beliefs and the feeling of betrayal by those whom we have trusted and considered friends.

Then I am reminded that you had similar moments of doubt and weariness. I even remember you commenting, in jest, how you thought there should be "a quota for suffering." Still, you said yes to the invitation to go beyond yourself, knowing fully well the formidable challenges that lay ahead. And I go back to that conversation we had in 2007, when we lamented the idea that there seemed to be no hope for our country, and you strongly urged us to never give up, not while we still had breath in our bodies.

When I compare my own trials with what you and Uncle Ninoy had gone through, I feel very humbled. Living as you did through a "time of great testing," as Fr. Frederik Fermin so aptly described it, you still managed to discover blessings behind your personal struggles. This realization has given me pause and helped me rediscover the blessings that I have tended to take for granted.

I cannot even begin to imagine the mental and emotional anguish you were undergoing during the years of Uncle Ninoy's imprisonment. Yet you looked back on this time as the most transformative chapter of your lives with a deep appreciation for the good that all the trials and sufferings yielded. Not only did your family become so much closer to each other, but Uncle Ninoy also became so much closer to God, while your faith strengthened even more as well. I recall you also mentioned that, in restrospect, dealing with all the hardships brought on by Uncle Ninoy's seven years and seven months in prison helped to steel you for his ultimate fate and granted you the courage and spirit to continue his unfinished mission.

From your life's example, I have come to realize that it is when we are emptied by the trials that have been brought upon us that we are reminded of the blessings that had filled us up in the first place and would fill us up again as we move on.

You and Uncle Ninoy endured and transcended all your trials because, amid the cruelty and unkindness of others, I saw how you, time and again, drew strength from your love for each another; from the love and sacrifice of your children, your parents, relatives, and true friends; and, more importantly, from the love of other unsung Filipinos who have also suffered and died for the same cause of freedom that you fought for side by side with them.

You engaged in so many battles. You won some, but you also lost many. When I come to think of it, both of you and innumerable others have left the world not seeing your dreams fully fulfilled. In the world's scorecard of success, you could actually be considered failures. Uncle Ninoy died without seeing democracy restored, and you left without seeing democracy being more relevant and beneficial to the vast majority of our people who remain poor and marginalized. It might also be said that even Jesus Christ, who died on the cross to save us from our sins, also left the world a seeming failure because mankind continues to sin to this day. But, moved by His love, His disciples lovingly also carried their own crosses for others, trusting that those they touched would do the same.

In your case, it also gives me much consolation and inspiration that there are still many of us who have carried on what you have not finished. If only for that, I can say that your sacrifices have not gone to waste.

I remember you once told me to stop worrying too much about what other people have to say about us, whether good or bad. I remember you reproached me and told me not to bother people about giving you a birthday tribute and, instead, simply concentrate on doing what we need to do for our people, whether it is appreciated or not.

Seeing how your life has touched so many people in a profound way, you have taught me that when we sincerely choose to be part of other people's lives and be truly present in their struggles, somehow there will be some who will also be moved to be part of ours and, more importantly, of other people's lives as well. You have also made me surrender to the reality, with much peace in my heart, that over time we may even be totally forgotten; but what would never be forgotten is the feeling of being loved.

Love continues to grow in the world despite the noise of hate, and that gives me much hope.

Someone loved us first

I also recall the time you were told by a nun that the Lord dispenses suffering to those that He loves. And you remarked, good-humoredly, "Maybe the Lord should not love me too much!"

The thing is, you and Uncle Ninoy have reminded me that the Lord still chooses to love us even if we do not ask to be loved. In fact, He even gives us the freedom to choose to love Him in return or not. Uncle Ninoy's transformation story in Laur reminded me that we often do not recognize and feel His love especially during very difficult times in our lives. Sometimes, we even feel abandoned during those tough moments when we need Him most. But, as you and Uncle Ninoy would always point out, He actually never leaves us. We merely fail to recognize Him in people who come into our lives, whether they are there to lend us a helping hand or even just to comfort us with their quiet presence. They can also be someone who happens to randomly say or casually do something that suddenly humbles us, teaches us, and encourages us to be the better person that we can be. They could be our spouse, our children, our parents, our siblings, our relatives, our friends, our boss, our staff or co-worker, a nun or a priest, our teacher or schoolmate, our household help or driver, a total stranger whom we may encounter as we go through our every day, or, even, those who oppose and persecute us.

Somehow, I am relieved knowing that not all of us are called to live lives like you and Uncle Ninoy had lived. But if there is one thing we have in common with both of you, it's that we are all called to make choices in our lives that can profoundly transform us and others who become part of our lives.

Thank you, again, Auntie Cory, for giving me the opportunity and the privilege to witness up close how you loved the people that the Lord brought into your life in the same way He loved you—unconditionally.

Please pray and intercede for me that I may be constantly ready and willing to share my gifts and do the best I can in the remaining time He has blessed me with.

Please be patient with me, as I know I will still fall and fail many times.

When these moments of weakness come my way, please never stop reminding me to follow your way, that I may always choose to love another day.

KEY NAMES

Agrava, Corazon Juliano

A retired court of appeals justice who was appointed to head the board that replaced Chief Justice Enrique Fernando's commission tasked to investigate Ninoy Aquino's assassination.

Almonte, Jose "Joe"

Retired general who helped establish the Reform the Armed Forces Movement (RAM). Prior to the People Power I Revolution, he held numerous security and intelligence posts. He retired from the Armed Forces in 1986 but was then appointed by Pres. Cory Aquino to head the National Intelligence Coordinating Agency.

Alvarez, Heherson "Sonny"

Co-founded Movement for a Free Philippines and served as its secretary-general.

Apostol, Eugenia "Eggie" Duran

Publisher of *Mr. & Ms. Magazine* who also co-founded the *Philippine Daily Inquirer* in 1985.

Aquino, Agapito "Butz"

Son of Benigno Simeon Aquino, Sr. and Aurora Aquino and younger brother of Ninoy Aquino. He was one of the founders of the August Twenty-One Movement (ATOM) and later served as senator from 1998 to 2007.

Aquino, Benigno Simeon "Noynoy" Cojuangco, III

Third child and only son of Ninoy and Cory Aquino. He would later serve as congressman for the second district of Tarlac Province (1998 to 2007), senator (2007 to 2010), and the fifteenth president of the Republic of the Philippines (2010 to 2016).

Aquino, Doña Aurora Lampa

Mother of Ninoy Aquino.

Aquino, Kristina Bernadette "Kris" Cojuangco

Youngest child of Ninoy and Cory Aquino.

Aquino, Paul	Son of Benigno Simeon Aquino, Sr. and Aurora Aquino and younger brother of Ninoy Aquino.
Aquino-Abellada, Aurora Corazon "Pinky"	Second daughter of Ninoy and Cory Aquino.
Aquino-Cruz, Maria Elena "Ballsy"	Eldest child of Ninoy and Cory Aquino.
Aquino-Dee, Victoria Elisa "Viel"	Third daughter of Ninoy and Cory Aquino.
Aragon, Fritzi Ruiz	Assistant to Pres. Cory Aquino.
Arevalo, Catalino, S.J.	Jesuit theologian and spiritual adviser of Pres. Cory Aquino.
Arguelles, Guido, S.J.	Jesuit priest who rallied against the Marcos dictatorship in the streets and in his on-air programs on Radio Veritas.
Armacost, Michael	US ambassador to the Philippines at the time of Ninoy's assassination.
Arroyo, Ceferino "Joker", Jr.	Politician and human rights lawyer who was one of the legal counsels of Ninoy Aquino at his military tribunal trial. He would later on become executive secretary of Pres. Cory Aquino.
Ayala, Jesus "Chito"	Mindanao-based businessman who supported the anti-dictatorship movement, and a friend of the Aquinos'. His knowledge and experience in Mindanao were invaluable to many politicians outside of the region.
Bangkok Post	The only English-language newspaper in Bangkok during Martial Law. Its editor-in-chief at the time, Theh Chongkhadikij, had known Ninoy Aquino since the latter's days as a journalist.
Barbero, Carmelo "Mike"	Deputy defense minister in 1976.
Barican, Fernando "Gerry"	Lawyer and student activist who later became a banker and political analyst.

"Bayan Ko"

A song originally written during the American occupation of the Philippines and sung in opposition to them. It was resurrected during Martial Law and became the unofficial anthem of protest against the Marcos dictatorship.

Bengzon, Alfredo R.A. "Alran"

A medical doctor who later became the secretary of health under Pres. Cory Aquino. He was instrumental in the establishment of the Convenor Group.

Benigno, Teodoro "Teddy", Jr.

A journalist who also served as Manila bureau chief of the Agence France-Presse from 1962 to 1987. He helped establish the Foreign Correspondents Association of the Philippines during Martial Law and would later become Pres. Cory Aquino's press secretary and a close friend until his death in 2005.

Bernas, Joaquin, S.J.

Jesuit priest and lawyer specializing in the Philippine constitution. He was appointed member of the Constitutional Commission in 1986.

Bicutan

Bicutan, a large land area that traverses Taguig City and Parañaque City, was associated with one of the main detention centers during Martial Law, Camp Bagong Diwa, as it hosted the said detention center.

Boncayao, Alex

Labor rights advocate who ran under the Lakas ng Bayan (LABAN) slate in the 1978 Interim Batasang Pambansa elections. He was killed by Philippine government security forces in 1983. In May 1984, an urban assassination unit of the communist New People's Army (NPA), called the Alex Boncayao Brigade, was organized and named after him.

Bosworth, Stephen "Steve"

U.S. ambassador to the Philippines from 1984 to 1987.

Brizuela, Martin "Noy"

A friend of Ninoy Aquino's who accompanied him on his flight back to Manila in 1983.

Burton, Sandra	A correspondent for *Time* magazine known for her reporting on Pres. Ferdinand E. Marcos and on the assassination of Ninoy Aquino. She was on the same China Airlines flight with Aquino before the latter was assassinated.
Camp General Emilio Aguinaldo	Military headquarters of the Armed Forces of the Philippines. Located along EDSA and across Camp Crame, it became one of the main rally points during the EDSA (or People Power I) Revolution in 1986.
Camp Rafael T. Crame	One of the main detention centers during Martial Law and headquarters of the Philippine Constabulary. Located along EDSA and across Camp Aguinaldo, it became one of the main rally points during the EDSA (or People Power I) Revolution in 1986. Today, it is the general headquarters of the Philippine National Police.
Catholic Bishops Conference of the Philippines (CBCP)	Association of all diocesan Catholic bishops across the Philippines.
Claver, Francisco F., S.J.	Jesuit priest who fought against the imposition of martial law and protested human rights violations.
Cojuangco, Don Jose	Father of Cory Aquino.
Cojuangco, Doña Demetria "Metring" Sumulong	Mother of Cory Aquino.
Cojuangco, Jose "Peping"	The younger of two sons of Jose and Demetria Cojuangco and the youngest brother of Cory Aquino.
Collas, Juan "Johnny"	Filipino lawyer based in the US and brother of Winnie Monsod.
Commander Melody	Alias of NPA leader Benjamin Bie.

Concepcion, Jose "Joe", Jr.	A prominent businessman who, during Martial Law, helped establish the National Citizens' Movement for Free Elections (NAMFREL) and became its founding chairman. Pres. Cory Aquino would later appoint him secretary of trade, a position he held from 1986 to 1991.
Coseteng, Regina "Reggie" Sy	Close, childhood friend of Cory Aquino's.
Cruz, Eldon	Business executive and husband of Ballsy Aquino.
Cuenco, Antonio "Tony"	Politician from a prominent Cebu City family who supported Cory Aquino's campaign.
Cunanan, Belinda Olivares	Journalist who helped establish the *Philippine Daily Inquirer*.
Daluz, Nenita "Inday Nita" Cortes	A well-known radio personality from Cebu who spoke out against the Marcos administration in her shows on air. She later became a member of parliament.
del Rosario, Ramon, V., Sr.	A well-known businessman and friend of the Aquinos'.
dela Costa, Horacio, S.J.	Jesuit priest and first Filipino provincial superior of the Society of Jesus.
Diokno, Carmen "Nena" Reyes Icasiano	Wife of Sen. Pepe Diokno. While her husband was detained, she petitioned for habeas corpus on his behalf and visited him every day in his cell.
Diokno, Jose "Pepe"	Secretary of justice to Pres. Diosdado Macapagal in 1962. He then ran for senator and served from 1963 until 1972, when his second term was cut short by the declaration of martial law. He was arrested with no charges and was among those detained in Fort Bonifacio and Fort Magsaysay with Ninoy. After his release in 1974, he dedicated his life to promoting and protecting human rights and Philippine sovereignty until his death in 1987.

Face the Nation

A local TV talk show broadcasted on the government network GTV-4.

Fermin, Frederik, OP

A Dominican priest who served as rector of the University of Santo Tomas from 1978 to 1982.

Fernando, Enrique

Appointed by President Marcos as the eightieth associate justice of the Supreme Court of the Philippines from 1967 to 1979 and thirteenth chief justice from 1979 to 1985. His assignment to head the commission to investigate Ninoy's assassination was controversial since it violated the constitutional separation of powers and, because he was appointed by Marcos, there were concerns that the investigation would not be independent. His commission was dissolved shortly and was replaced by a new one headed by Corazon Agrava.

Fort Bonifacio

One of the detention centers for political prisoners during Martial Law and the headquarters of the Philippine Army and the Philippine Marines.

Fort Magsaysay

Largest military reserve in the Philippines located in Laur, Nueva Ecija. It was where Ninoy Aquino and Pepe Diokno were detained after Ninoy managed to have anti-Marcos and anti-martial law articles published in the *Bangkok Post.*

Galman, Rolando

Alleged assassin of Ninoy Aquino who was gunned down by security forces immediately after he allegedly shot Ninoy.

Garcia, Enrique Voltaire, II

Student activist, lawyer, and congressman. He was among those arrested and detained in Fort Bonifacio with Ninoy. After a brief period of detention, he was placed under house arrest but lost his battle to leukemia in 1973.

Gazmin, Voltaire	As a young lieutenant, he was one of the officers assigned to secure the detention facility in Fort Magsaysay where Ninoy Aquino and Pepe Diokno were detained. He later served as Pres. Cory Aquino's head of the Presidential Security Group. He would be given multiple honors in his career. He was appointed commanding general of the Philippine Army in 1999 and Philippine ambassador to Cambodia in 2002, before becoming secretary of national defense under Pres. Benigno Simeon C. Aquino III, Pres. Cory Aquino's son.
Go-Belmonte, Betty	A journalist and publisher who established the STAR group of news publications. During Martial Law, she started *The Star*, an opposition monthly magazine. In 1985, she, along with Eggie Apostol and Max Soliven, founded the *Philippine Daily Inquirer*. On July 28, 1986, she, together with Max Soliven and Art Borjal, established *The Philippine Star*.
Golez, Jose Roilo	A former navy officer and a veteran legislator. He served as postmaster general under Pres. Ferdinand Marcos and was national security adviser under Pres. Gloria Macapagal-Arroyo.
Gonzales, Neptali	A lawyer and one of the legal counsels of Ninoy Aquino during his military tribunal trial in 1975. He would later become secretary of justice under Pres. Cory Aquino and a senator.
Gonzales, Tony	A journalist and family friend of the Aquinos'. He would later become one of the founders of the Benigno S. Aquino, Jr. Foundation and minister of tourism under Pres. Cory Aquino.
Guingona, Ruth de Lara	Politician from Mindanao and wife of Tito Guingona.
Guingona, Teofisto "Tito", Jr.	A delegate to the 1971 Constitutional Convention. During Martial Law, he was jailed twice for his opposition to the government. He later became chairman of the Commission on Audit under Pres. Cory Aquino, senator from 1987 to 1993, and held various other government positions thereafter.

Habib, Philip

American diplomat who was sent by then-US Pres. Ronald Reagan to mediate a possible power-sharing agreement between Ferdinand Marcos and Cory Aquino after both declared their victory in the 1986 presidential elections.

Herrera, Trinidad "Trining"

Community organizer and advocate for the urban poor. During Martial Law, she was arrested, detained, and tortured many times for trying to protect communities from being demolished for the Marcoses' urban projects.

Honrado, Angel "Bodet"

Retired Philippine Air Force general who previously served as commanding officer of the Presidential Security Group of Pres. Cory Aquino and general manager of the Manila International Airport Authority under Pres. Noynoy Aquino.

Ileto, Rafael "Rocky"

He was one of the few generals who opposed Pres. Ferdinand Marcos and his declaration of martial law. Under Pres. Cory Aquino, he served as undersecretary of defense before becoming secretary of national defense.

Interim Batasang Pambansa Elections

Held in 1978 to elect the representatives to the country's first parliament.

Ishihara, Shintaro

Member of the House of Representatives of Japan at the time of Ninoy Aquino's assassination. He was also governor of Tokyo from 1999 to 2012. He was a close friend of the Aquinos'.

Javier, Evelio

Served as governor of the province of Antique and a leader of Cory Aquino's campaign in his home province. He was assassinated just days after the snap elections while monitoring the canvassing of election returns.

Kalaw, Eva Estrada

A senator from 1965 to 1972 before her term was cut short by the declaration of martial law. She was one of the strongest opposition figures during Martial Law and was imprisoned twice in Fort Bonifacio. She was a second cousin of Ninoy Aquino's.

Kalaw-Puyat, Saturnina "Nina" Estrada	A well-known Filipino writer. She was a second cousin of Ninoy's and sister of Eva. Her husband's family, owner of the Loyola Memorial Chapels, volunteered to help with Ninoy's funeral arrangements.
Karingal, Tomas	Brigadier general and former police chief of Quezon City.
Kashiwahara, Ken	Journalist for ABC News who accompanied Ninoy on his flight back to Manila in 1983. He is the husband of Lupita, sister of Ninoy.
Kashiwahara, Lupita Aquino	Daughter of Benigno Simeon Aquino, Sr. and Aurora Aquino and younger sister of Ninoy.
Kilusang Bagong Lipunan (KBL)	A political party in the Philippines initially formed in 1978 as a coalition of parties supporting President Marcos for the Interim Batasang Pambansa elections. The party eventually became President Marcos's political machinery during Martial Law.
Lakas ng Bayan (LABAN)	The opposition political party led by detained opposition leader Ninoy Aquino and established in 1978 for the Interim Batasang Pambansa elections.
Laurel, Jose Bayani "Pepito", Jr.	Speaker of the House of Representatives, from 1967 to 1971, under Pres. Ferdinand Marcos. He was the brother of former vice-president Salvador "Doy" Laurel and former ambassador Jose Sotero "Pepe" Laurel.
Laurel, Jose Sotero "Pepe"	Ambassador of the Philippines to Japan, from 1966 to 1971. He was the brother of Doy Laurel and former speaker Pepito Laurel.
Laurel, Salvador Roman "Doy"	A senator from 1967 to 1972 until his term was cut short by the declaration of martial law. He later served as vice-president to Cory Aquino. He was the brother of former speaker Pepito Laurel and former ambassador Pepe Laurel.

Legaspi, Leonardo	Former Caceres archbishop and first Filipino rector of the University of Santo Tomas.
Liberal Party (LP)	Second oldest active political party in the Philippines. It began as a liberal group that broke away from the larger Nacionalista Party. President Marcos was a member of the LP and served as its president from 1961 to 1964 before going back to the Nacionalista Party. During Marcos's presidency, the party became the voice of the opposition, challenging Marcos on issues concerning human rights and democracy. Many of its members were detained and killed during Martial Law.
Lichauco, Ernesto "Esto"	The husband of Maur Aquino and brother-in-law of Ninoy Aquino.
Lichauco, Maria Aurora "Maur" Aquino	First child of Benigno Simeon Aquino, Sr. and Aurora Aquino and elder sister of Ninoy Aquino.
Locsin, Teodoro "Teddy", Sr.	A journalist and publisher of *The Philippines Free Press,* one of the publications critical of the Marcos administration. He was the father of Teodoro "Teddy Boy" Locsin, Jr.
Locsin, Teodoro "Teddy Boy", Jr.	A journalist and a son of Teddy Locsin, Sr. He was the presidential adviser and speech-writer of Pres. Cory Aquino. He would later become a congressman in Makati City and the secretary of foreign affairs under Pres. Rodrigo Duterte.
Lopa, Ricardo "Baby"	Father of the author and husband of Terry Cojuangco-Lopa.
Lopa, Teresita "Terry" Cojuangco	Mother of the author. She is the third child of Jose and Demetria Cojuangco and the older sister of Cory Aquino.
Lopez, Conchita "Chita" La'O	Wife of Geny Lopez.
Lopez, Consuelo "Connie" Rufino	Wife of Oscar "Oski" Lopez and a close friend of Cory Aquino's.

Lopez, Eugenio "Geny", Jr.

Businessman and then-heir to the Lopez family's business empire. When martial law was declared, he was arrested and accused of conspiring with Serge Osmeña III to assassinate Marcos. He became close friends with Serge during their incarceration. In November 1974, he and Serge went on a hunger strike to protest the unjust detention of innocent Filipinos. This resulted in the release of over a thousand political prisoners. In 1977, he and Serge escaped from Fort Bonifacio and went into exile in the US. There, they continued organizing movements against Marcos.

Lopez, Fernando "Nanding", Sr.

Marcos's vice-president from 1965 to 1972. He was the uncle of Geny and Oski.

Lopez, Oscar "Oski"

Businessman and younger brother of Eugenio "Geny" Lopez.

Lopez, Tony

A senior correspondent of *Asiaweek*, a Hong Kong-based weekly magazine.

Lucman, Haroun Rashid

Politician from Lanao del Sur and friend of Ninoy Aquino's. He called for the impeachment of Pres. Ferdinand Marcos in 1968, citing the president's responsibility regarding the Jabidah massacre. When martial law was declared, he went into exile in Saudi Arabia. In 1980, Ninoy and Rashid were reunited in exile and started working on plans for Moro autonomy.

Lugar, Richard

American Republican senator who served from 1977 to 2013. He led a group of US Congressional observers in the Philippines for the 1986 snap elections. Later, he supported the presidency of Cory Aquino.

Macapagal-Arroyo, Gloria

President of the Republic of the Philippines from January 2001 to June 2010.

Maceda, Ernesto "Ernie"	A senator from 1971 to 1972 and 1987 to 1998. He held various positions during President Marcos's term before he became senator. When martial law was declared, he broke away from Marcos and went into exile in the US. He would become one of Ninoy's advisers and, after Ninoy's assassination, one of the leaders of the opposition.
Malloch-Brown, Mark	Political strategist. During Cory Aquino's election campaign, he was the lead international partner at Sawyer-Miller, a political and communications consulting firm.
Manglapus, Raul	Co-founded and headed the Movement for a Free Philippines. He was also a brother-in-law of Geny Lopez through their wives, Pacita and Conchita La'O, who were sisters.
Marcos, Ferdinand	The tenth president of the Philippines who extended his rule by declaring martial law (1972 to 1986). He had been president since 1965.
Marcos, Imelda Romualdez	Wife of Ferdinand Marcos.
Mathay, Ismael "Mel" A., Jr.	Vice-governor of the Metro Manila Commission (today's Metropolitan Manila Development Authority or MMDA) under President Marcos.
Mendoza, Estelito	Solicitor general to President Marcos until the People Power I Revolution. He would later represent Imelda Marcos and a number of officials accused of graft and corruption.
Misuari, Nur	Moro revolutionary and politician who founded the Moro National Liberation Front.
Mitra, Ramon "Monching", Jr.	A senator from 1971 to 1972 before his term was cut short by the declaration of martial law. He would later run for the Interim Batasang Pambansa in 1978, together with Ninoy Aquino. In 1984 he was elected assemblyman to the Regular Batasang Pambansa. He would later serve as Pres. Cory Aquino's agriculture minister and speaker of the House of Representatives from 1987to 1992 when he was congressman for the second district of Palawan.

Monsod, Solita "Winnie" Collas	Economist and broadcaster. She would later become Pres. Cory Aquino's National Economic and Development Authority director general from 1987 to 1989.
Montelibano, Maria	Niece of Ninoy and Cory Aquino and former head of Radio Television Malacañang (RTVM).
Movement for a Free Philippines	Opposition group against martial law and Marcos's dictatorship based in San Francisco, California, USA.
Mr. and Ms. Magazine	Weekly tabloid created by publisher Eugenia Apostol to publish news and articles in opposition to martial law and Marcos's dictatorship.
Muñoz-Palma, Cecilia "Celing"	Appointed associate justice of the Supreme Court of the Philippines from 1973 to 1978. During her term, she spoke against injustice and human rights violations, which prompted Sen. Jose W. Diokno's release after four years in detention and the transfer of Ninoy Aquino's case from a military to a civilian court. In 1986, Pres. Cory Aquino appointed her as a member of the Constitutional Commission, where she led the crafting of the 1987 constitution as the commission's president.
Mydans, Seth	Journalist and correspondent for *The New York Times, Newsweek,* and the Associated Press. He covered the People Power I Revolution, including the elections, in 1986.
National Citizens' Movement for Free Elections (NAMFREL)	Established in 1983 as a citizenry-led and non-partisan election monitoring body. In the 1986 snap elections, the Commission on Elections recognized NAMFREL as its citizens' arm. Their parallel, manual count of the snap election votes showed that it was Cory Aquino who won and not Ferdinand Marcos, who nonetheless declared himself winner of the elections.
New People's Army (NPA)	Armed wing of the Communist Party of the Philippines.

Ninoy and Cory Aquino Foundation (NCAF)	Originally established in 1983 as the Benigno S. Aquino, Jr. Foundation (BSAF) by Cory Aquino to perpetuate his legacy. After Cory Aquino passed away in 2009, the foundation was renamed Ninoy and Cory Aquino Foundation to empower the people to follow their lives of self-sacrifice and self-transcendence in service to humanity.
Olaguer, Antonio "Toti", S.J.	Jesuit priest who fought against the Marcos dictatorship and was arrested and detained during Martial Law for rebellion.
Ongpin, Jaime "Jimmy"	A prominent businessman and president of the Philippines' oldest mining company, Benguet Corporation. He would later on become minister of finance under Pres. Cory Aquino.
Oreta, Antolin "Len" M., Jr.	A politician who, during Martial Law, was arrested and detained for rebellion against the government. He is the brother-in-law of Ninoy Aquino.
Oreta, Maria Teresa "Tessie" Aquino	The youngest sister of Ninoy Aquino and wife of Len Oreta.
Osmeña, John Henry	A senator from 1971 to 1972, 1987 to 1995, and 1998 to 2004. He is a grandson of the fourth president of the Philippines, Sergio Osmeña, Sr. When martial law was declared, he went into exile to the US.
Osmeña, Marilita	Former wife of Sergio "Serge" Osmeña III.
Osmeña, Sergio "Serge", III	He is a grandson of the fourth president of the Philippines, Sergio Osmeña, Sr. He was imprisoned during the dictatorship on charges of conspiring with Geny Lopez to assassinate Marcos. He became a senator in 1995.
Osmeña-Stuart, Maria Victoria "Minnie"	Politician from Cebu and sister of Serge Osmeña III.
Pauker, Guy	Intelligence analyst from Rand Corporation who specialized in Asia.

People Power I or EDSA I Revolution	The non-violent people's protests in the Philippines that occurred in February 1986 and that led to the departure of Pres. Ferdinand Marcos, ending his twenty-one-year dictatorship and restoring democracy in the Philippines. Most of the protests occurred along Epifanio de los Santos Avenue (EDSA).
People Power II or EDSA II Revolution	A similar people's action that led to the transfer of leadership from then-Pres. Joseph E. Estrada to then-Vice Pres. Gloria Macapagal-Arroyo in January 2001, after the former was forced to relinquish power due to corruption issues raised against him.
Perez, Bernardo Maria "Bobby", OSB or Perez, Rodrigo, III	Benedictine monk and former rector of San Beda College.
Pimentel, Aquilino "Nene", Jr.	A politician and lawyer, he rose to the national arena as a delegate to the 1971 Constitutional Convention. He was arrested and detained in 1973 for opposing a Marcos-washed constitution. He ran for a position in the Interim Batasang Pambansa elections under the LABAN party but lost, along with the other opposition candidates. He took part in a protest of the elections and was arrested once more. He would later become mayor of Cagayan de Oro despite Martial Law and interference from Marcos. He would be charged and arrested many times over but would continue the fight. After the People Power I Revolution, Pres. Cory Aquino appointed him minister of local government before he ran for the Senate in 1987. He was a senator from 1987 to 1992 and 1998 to 2010.
Pimentel, Lourdes "Bing" de la Llana	Wife of Nene Pimentel.
Pink Sisters or Holy Spirit Adoration Sisters	A Roman Catholic institute of contemplative, cloistered nuns known for wearing pink-colored habits. Cory Aquino was particularly close to the Pink Sisters because of her frequent visits to their convent and devotion to Mary.

Planas, Rosario "Charito"

Politician who led a campaign against the 1973 constitution. Upon the declaration of martial law, she was arrested and detained along with other opposition leaders. She ran for a position in the Interim Batasang Pambansa elections under the LABAN party but lost, along with the other opposition candidates. After the elections, she left for the US and joined the anti-Marcos movement there until after the 1986 People Power I Revolution.

Policarpio, Alfonso "Poli", Jr.

Close friend of Ninoy Aquino's and a senior executive assistant to him.

Police Constabulary (PC)

A police force in the Philippines in 1901 that eventually became part of the military. The PC was one of the main law enforcement bodies to arrest, detain, and torture oppositionists during the martial law administration of President Marcos. Following the crafting of the 1987 constitution, the PC was merged with the Integrated National Police, which would become the Philippine National Police (PNP) today.

Ponce Enrile, Juan "Johnny", Sr.

One of the closest allies and a protégé of President Marcos's. He served as President Marcos's secretary of justice (1968 to1970) and minister of defense (1972 to 1986). Later, in 1986, he would shift alliances and become one of the key figures in the People Power I Revolution. He would then go on to become a congressman and senator for multiple terms. His career is marred by many controversies and charges of graft and corruption.

Psinakis, Steve

Brother-in-law of Geny Lopez.

Radio Veritas

Catholic radio station that was the only news outlet that covered live the assassination and funeral of Ninoy Aquino and was instrumental in mobilizing people to join the 1986 People Power I Revolution.

Rama, Napoleon "Nap"	A journalist for *The Philippines Free Press* and publisher of *The Manila Times*. He served as an opposition delegate to the 1971 Constitutional Convention and was among those detained in Fort Bonifacio with Ninoy. He would later found the Cory Aquino for President Movement (CAPM) in 1985.
Ramas, Josephus	Commanding general of the Philippine Army from 1981 to 1986.
Ramos, Fidel "Eddie"	Before becoming the twelfth president of the Philippines, he headed the Philippine Constabulary during Martial Law and would later become the vice-chief of staff of the Armed Forces of the Philippines. He would later break away from the Marcos administration and shift alliances to Cory Aquino during the 1986 People Power I Revolution. He was subsequently appointed chief of staff of the Armed Forces of the Philippines and secretary of national defense under Pres. Cory Aquino.
Reform the Armed Forces Movement (RAM)	Military group that served as the backbone of the rebellion triggering the People Power I Revolution in 1986.
Reyes, Gabriel "Gabby"	Bishop emeritus of Antipolo who was the protégé of Cardinal Sin. He was the main driver of the construction of the EDSA Shrine after Martial Law.
Reyes, Josephine Cojuangco	Second child of Jose and Demetria Cojuangco and the eldest sister of Cory Aquino.
Roces, Joaquin "Chino"	A journalist, founder, and publisher of *The Manila Times*. One of the many arrested in 1972 shortly after the declaration of martial law. He was a family friend of the Cojuangcos' and Aquinos' and would later initiate the gathering of one million signatures to petition Cory Aquino to run for president.
Roces, Pacita Carvajal	Wife of Chino Roces.

Rodrigo, Francisco "Soc"	Senator, playwright, broadcaster, and lawyer who worked in the law firm of Sen. Lorenzo Tañada before Martial Law. He was among those detained with Ninoy. He was released after three months but detained twice more for writing poems against the Marcos dictatorship. He would later become one of the commissioners of the Constitutional Commission who would frame the new 1987 Philippine constitution after the People Power I Revolution.
Romualdez, Benjamin "Kokoy"	Younger brother of Imelda Marcos. His brother-in-law, President Marcos, appointed him ambassador to various countries while concurrently serving as governor of Leyte Province. The Presidential Commission on Good Government (PCGG), tasked to recover ill-gotten wealth from the Marcoses after the lifting of martial law, listed Kokoy as one of the Marcos relatives who allegedly acquired several companies illegally.
Roxas, Gerardo "Gerry", Sr.	A senator from 1963 to 1972, until his term was cut short by the declaration of martial law. During Martial Law, he was the leader of two major opposition bodies: he was president of the Liberal Party and co-chairman of the United Nationalist Democratic Organization (UNIDO). He was the son of the fifth president of the Philippines, Manuel Acuña Roxas.
Roxas, Judy Araneta	Wife of Gerry Roxas.
Saguisag, Rene	A lawyer and lawmaker. During Martial Law, he took on cases of human rights victims who could not afford legal services. A close friend of Ninoy Aquino's, he would later become one of the senior counsels of Cory Aquino during her campaign for presidency. After her win, he was appointed presidential spokesperson, a position he held until he ran for the Senate. He served as senator from 1987 to 1992.

Salonga, Jovito "Jovy"	A senator. He was among those detained in Fort Bonifacio with Ninoy.
San Gabriel, Jose "Pepot"	Family doctor of the Aquinos'.
Shaplen, Robert "Bob"	An American journalist and correspondent for *The New Yorker* who covered the Asia region during Martial Law.
Sin, Jaime	Catholic archbishop of Manila and a cardinal. He was instrumental in rallying the people during the People Power Revolutions in 1986 and 2001.
Solis, Rolando "Rolly"	A Filipino-American cardiologist and a family friend of the Aquinos'. He is based in Baylor University Medical Center in Dallas, Texas, where Ninoy underwent surgery.
Soliven, Maximo "Max"	A journalist who was among those detained in Fort Bonifacio with Ninoy. He would later co-found *The Philippine Daily Inquirer* in 1985 and *Philippine Star* in 1986, where he was the publisher until his death in 2006.
Soliven, Preciosa Silverio	Wife of Max Soliven.
Syjuco, Jose	Brigadier general who headed the second military tribunal/commission.
Tan, Christine	A nun from the Religious of the Good Shepherd and an activist. She was a friend of Cory Aquino's and was appointed a member of the Constitutional Commission in 1986.
Tañada, Lorenzo, Sr.	A lawyer and senator who represented many human rights victims and those wrongfully detained, including Ninoy Aquino. In 1978, he became the campaign manager for the LABAN party's run in the Interim Batasang Pambansa elections. It was he who gave Ninoy hope in the darkest days of his incarceration, and who kept Ninoy updated on the state of the Philippines when the Aquino family lived in Boston.

Taruc, Luis

Leader of Hukbalahap (Hukbong Bayan Laban sa Hapon), popularly known as the "Huks," a socialist and communist guerrilla movement that started out in 1942 as a rebellion against the Japanese during their occupation of the Philippines but later also put up a rebellion against the Philippine government. He was pardoned by President Marcos in 1968 after serving just fourteen years of four life sentences.

Tatad, Francisco "Kit"

President Marcos's minister of public information from 1969 to 1980. He became senator from 1992 up to 2001.

Tayag, Nilo

Bishop of the Philippine Independent Church. He co-founded the communist group Kabataang Makabayan in 1964. He was the group's national chairman until he was arrested in 1970. He pleaded guilty to the charge of subversion and was released in 1982.

Teehankee, Claudio

Chief justice of the Supreme Court of the Philippines from 1987 to 1988. Although he was appointed as an associate justice by President Marcos, he was a staunch defender of civil rights who challenged the 1973 constitution. He swore in Pres. Cory Aquino after the 1986 snap elections and was appointed as chief justice. Before his retirement in 1988, he ordered a retrial of Ninoy Aquino's murder case.

Teopaco, Maria Paz "Passy" Cojuangco

Youngest child of Jose and Demetria Cojuangco and the youngest sister of Cory Aquino.

United Nationalist Democratic Organization (UNIDO)

The foremost opposition coalition of parties against the administration of Pres. Ferdinand Marcos formed in 1980.

University Belt

An unofficial name for the area in Manila where many colleges and universities are located. It is near Malacañang Palace and, thus, a place where protesters often go through to protest near the Palace.

Upsilon Sigma Phi	Oldest fraternity in the Philippines.
Velez, Jose Mari	Lawyer, journalist, and businessman. He served as an opposition delegate to the 1971 Constitutional Convention and was among those arrested and detained in Fort Bonifacio with Ninoy Aquino shortly after martial law was declared.
Ver, Fabian	General and chief of staff of the Armed Forces of the Philippines from 1981 to1984 and 1985 to 1986. He was a cousin of President Marcos's.
Viewpoint	A public affairs TV talk show broadcasted on the GMA network.
Villafuerte, Luis, Sr.	Politician and President Marcos's minister of trade from 1979 to 1981.
Villegas, Bernardo "Bernie"	A writer and economist who was a member of the Constitutional Commission that would frame the new 1987 Philippine constitution after the People Power I Revolution.
Wakamiya, Kiyoshi	Japanese journalist who accompanied Ninoy Aquino on his flight to Manila in 1983. He was an eyewitness to Ninoy's assassination.
Women's Auxiliary Corps (WAC)	Non-combat/administrative arm of the military staffed by women.

INDEX

ACKNOWLEDGMENTS

To Love Another Day would not have been possible if Fr. Catalino Arevalo, S.J., did not first broach the idea of this book around eight years ago. Let me therefore use this opportunity to once again thank Father Arevalo for believing in me when I myself did not.

Father Arevalo's constant and patient encouragement, year after year, whenever we celebrated the death anniversaries of Auntie Cory and Uncle Ninoy, reminded me of a loving God who never gives up on me, even if, time and again, I ignored his proddings to use my gifts so I may share His love with others.

As I was putting this book together, I was also reminded that my limited gifts must never stop me from facing challenges that I initially found intimidating and daunting, such as the ability to write. I realized that there are always others around me who are more than willing to share their own gifts because we believe in the same causes and dreams.

Twenty-three years ago, my cousin, Rhona Lopa-Macasaet, was already a collaborator when we interviewed Auntie Cory to capture her stories, which are now enshrined in this book. Rhona painstakingly transcribed, edited, and preserved Auntie Cory's precious narrations, serving as their guardian and safe keeper until we resurrected them in May 2019. When I asked her about her edited transcripts and told her about my self-imposed deadline of launching the book by the end of the year, Rhona graciously offered to help me, even if she was busy editing two other books.

Mindful that I wanted the book to appeal to the younger generation, I am blessed to have my nephews Jamie Bautista and Paolo Reyes. They have each made their own mark in the publishing and media world, and helped me with the overall design, production, and editing of this book. I also wish to thank my assistant Pau Apines, who proofread the many drafts of the manuscript, carried out detailed research, and provided the curious lens of a young person who was not alive during those years. They also shared very useful insights on how best to present this material to their generation, who I hope would be inspired to do their share in building our nation.

I also wish to thank Alexander Loinaz for allowing us to use his photograph of Auntie Cory, taken on August 24, 1983, in Times Street, which became the basis for the cover artwork of this book. I will also be remiss if I did not single out my friend Mel Vera Cruz, my brother Jamike, and my wife Didi, who rendered their own painted portraits of Alex's photo and provided us with additional cover studies to choose from.

Of course, Didi's creativity is by no means her only contribution. She, together with our three children Andrea, Pia, and Carlo, provided me with unconditional love, patience, and support, without which I would never have been given the opportunity to journey with Auntie Cory for seventeen years. During those years, Didi would always assure Auntie Cory that she had fully accepted that my priorities were God, Country, Auntie Cory, and family.

Lastly, I cannot thank my cousins Ballsy, Pinky, Noy, Viel, and Kris enough for sharing their mom and dad with me, my family, our people, and our country. As Auntie Cory and Uncle Ninoy articulated in this book, their children shared their trials, struggles, burdens, and sacrifices. I know they could have easily chosen to live more quiet lives after their mom passed away. But as our history will testify, that was not the case.

ABOUT THE EDITOR

Rafael "Rapa" C. Lopa is the president and executive director of the Ninoy and Cory Aquino Foundation, Inc. and a senior advisor to the Office of the Vice President of the Philippines. He is the nephew of the late Pres. Corazon Cojuangco Aquino and served as her executive assistant for seventeen years, from 1993, when she stepped down from office, until her death in 2009. Together, they worked on a range of advocacies for social development, human rights, and political and governance reform. Driven by the leadership legacy of his aunt as well as the Jesuit formation of being "men for others," Lopa has dedicated his career to catalyzing collective action towards positive social change and sustainable development. Lopa also works as a management and development consultant, while also leading various organizations and projects that serve as platforms for nation building. He graduated from the Ateneo de Manila University in 1985 with a Bachelor of Arts degree in Interdisciplinary Studies.